HOW TO PASS ✓

STANDARD GRADE
COMPUTING
STUDIES

Frank Frame *and*
John Mason

Hodder Gibson
A MEMBER OF THE HODDER HEADLINE GROUP

The Publishers would like to thank the following for permission to reproduce copyright material:

Photo credits

Page 33 © Tibor Bognar/Alamy; page 47 © oote boe/Alamy; page 55 (left) © Microsoft product box shot reprinted with permission from Microsoft Corporation; page 55 (right) courtesy Larry Ewing lewing@isc.tamu.edu and The GIMP; page 59 © Jerry Mason/Science Photo Library; page 63 (top) © Chris Collins/Corbis; page 63 (bottom) © Hodder Education; page 64 (top) © Hodder Education; page 64 (bottom) © Esa Hiltula/Alamy; page 66 (all) © Hodder Education; page 67 (top) © Hodder Education; page 67 (bottom) © David Young-Wolff/Alamy; page 68 © James King-Holmes/W Industries/ Science Photo Library; page 69 (top) © Hodder Education; page 69 (bottom) © © 2006 Hewlett-Packard Development Company, L.P.; page 72 © Royalty-Free/Corbis; page 73 © Hodder Education; page 78 © Positive Image/Alamy; page 87 © The Moviestore Collection; page 91 © Paul Broadbent/Alamy; page 92 © Wernher Krutein/Alamy; page 93 © C. Moore/Corbis.

Acknowledgements

Every effort has been made to trace all copyright holders, but if any have been inadvertently overlooked the Publishers will be pleased to make the necessary arrangements at the first opportunity.

Although every effort has been made to ensure that website addresses are correct at time of going to press, Hodder Gibson cannot be held responsible for the content of any website mentioned in this book. It is sometimes possible to find a relocated web page by typing in the address of the home page for a website in the URL window of your browser.

Papers used in this book are natural, renewable and recyclable products. They are made from wood grown in sustainable forests. The logging and manufacturing processes conform to the environmental regulations of the country of origin.

Dedication

This book is dedicated to Edith and Jan, for without their limitless patience there would be no book – and we'd both be single!

JM and FF

Orders: please contact Bookpoint Ltd, 130 Milton Park, Abingdon, Oxon OX14 4SB. Telephone: (44) 01235 827720. Fax: (44) 01235 400454. Lines are open from 9.00 – 5.00, Monday to Saturday, with a 24-hour message answering service. Visit our website at www.hoddereducation.co.uk. Hodder Gibson can be contacted direct on: Tel: 0141 848 1609; Fax: 0141 889 6315; email: hoddergibson@hodder.co.uk

© Frank Frame and John Mason 2006
First published in 2006 by
Hodder Gibson, a member of the Hodder Headline Group
2a Christie Street
Paisley PA1 1NB

Impression number   10 9 8 7 6 5 4 3 2
Year   2010 2009 2008 2007

Cover photo Charlie Newham/Alamy
Typeset in 9.5/12.5pt Frutiger Light by Phoenix Photosetting, Chatham, Kent
Printed and bound in Great Britain by Martins The Printers, Berwick-upon-Tweed

A catalogue record for this title is available from the British Library

ISBN: 978-0-340-92650-5

CONTENTS

Introduction

This book is designed to help you pass Standard Grade Computing. The book covers all the topic areas in the course:

◆ General Purpose Packages

◆ Communications and Networks

◆ Computer Systems

◆ Commercial Data Processing

◆ Automated Systems.

The materials covers all the topics in the content grids in the SQA Standard Grade Computing arrangements document. Each chapter contains sets of questions covering the content of each topic, with marked sections for Credit level questions. A final chapter focuses on the external exam with information on the exam, tips on exam preparation and a set of exam style questions. Problem solving questions are also provided.

How to use this book

Use the book to check up on your knowledge of the topics on the checklist for each of the topics. Attempt all the questions. The answers are at the back of the book. Attempt all the problem solving questions and check the answers. Read the tips about exam preparation and come up with your own revision plan! Finally, attempt the exam style questions and check the answers.

If you do all this you will greatly improve your chances of passing Standard Grade Computing.

GENERAL PURPOSE PACKAGES

Key Words

- ★ General Purpose Packages
- ★ Human Computer Interface
- ★ data types
- ★ spreadsheets
- ★ graphics
- ★ presentation and multimedia
- ★ expert systems
- ★ storing data
- ★ software integration
- ★ word processing
- ★ databases
- ★ desktop publishing
- ★ web page creation
- ★ social, legal and economic implications

What are General Purpose Packages?

You need to know about the following General Purpose Packages:

- ◆ Word processing
- ◆ Graphics
- ◆ Web page creation
- Spreadsheets
- Integrated packages
- Desktop Publishing
- Databases
- Presentation and Multimedia
- Expert Systems

Why do we need General Purpose Packages?

We use computer systems and General Purpose Packages (GPPs) because they help us to **store**, **retrieve**, **manipulate** and **communicate** information. They also help us keep data **accurate**, **complete** and **up-to-date**. Computer systems with GPPs can be used to:

- ◆ **store** large volumes of information;
- ◆ **retrieve** information, to give you access to the information you have stored;
- ◆ **manipulate**, or change the content and the way information is presented;
- ◆ **communicate**, or send, the information to another person;
- ◆ ensure that information is **accurate** and correct;
- ◆ ensure that information is **complete** and there is nothing missing;
- ◆ ensure that information is **up-to-date** and can be regularly checked and changed if necessary.

The flow of information

In business, the movement of data within and between offices should be as efficient as possible. A computer system running GPPs can help achieve this.

◆ Files can be quickly **accessed** and **updated**.

◆ **Management Reports** can quickly be drawn up and distributed.

◆ Files can be **stored** on disc and quickly printed out for those who need it.

What type of data can you store using a GPP?

The data types that you are expected to know about are: numbers, text, graphics, audio and photographic data.

At Credit, we add animation and video data to the list as well!

Which GPP can you find these data types in? The latest GPP can handle all of these data types but video, audio and animation are most commonly found in multimedia, presentation and web page creation packages.

Data type	Packages
Text: characters, words, paragraphs	All packages
Graphics: Drawings, graphs, designs	All packages
Audio: Music tracks, voice-overs	All packages, but most commonly found in multimedia, presentation, web page creation
Animation: Moving graphics	Commonly found in multimedia, presentation, web page creation
Photographic: Photographs taken by a digital camera	All packages, but most commonly found in multimedia, presentation, web page creation
Video: Clips taken by digital camcorder or downloaded from the Internet	All packages, but most commonly found in multimedia, presentation, web page creation

Audio data

Many software packages can handle audio data. Audio data can be stored as MIDI files or as digital audio files.

A MIDI audio file stores a description of the sound, such as the type of instrument, pitch, volume and the length of a note. With this information the system can recreate a sound.

A digital audio file stores a digital copy of a sound, like a sample. This sample can then be manipulated to get the effect you are looking for. Details about exactly how this is done is covered in the systems chapter when we look at audio cards (see pages 68).

One problem with digital audio files is that they can be very large. Storing data in an uncompressed digital audio format, such as .WAV files, you can store approximately 70 minutes of music on a CD. If you compress the data, using the compressed MP3 file format, you can store ten times this amount on a single CD.

Photographic data

When you take a picture with a digital camera it stores a digital representation of the image. You can transfer this image to your computer and process it using graphics software. Exactly how this is done is covered in the systems chapter (see pages 67).

Like audio files, graphic images can be very large indeed, and they are often compressed before being stored and used.

Animation

GIF animation is a common way of creating animated graphics. To create the animated effect the software displays a series of still images, or frames, one after the other. To get a realistic level of animation 16 to 24 frames per second are needed. The computer has to store a binary number for each pixel on the screen and repeat this for every frame in the animation.

Uncompressed video images

When recording a video clip, the computer stores a bitmap image of each frame. This means that file sizes could be very large indeed. If you are recording at a speed of 25 frames per second and a single colour frame requires one megabyte, then the camera will have to store 25 Megabytes per second of video!

Compressed video footage

It is obvious that there is a need to compress the video images. If you didn't then you would find it very difficult to store and process them. Most video images are now compressed using the MPEG-2 format, which can compress the files to less than 2% of their original size.

Video images are manipulated in multimedia or video editing packages.

Backup

To guard against data loss you should make a copy of all your important data. This should be done regularly and the backup kept on a disk or tape separate from the original. This means that you can replace data that is lost or corrupted.

Standard file formats

We can save text documents in different file formats, such as ASCII, TXT or RTF.

Advantage

The advantage of using these standard formats is that they are recognised by a wide range of applications. This means that you can transfer text from one application to another.

ASCII (or TXT)

A file saved as an ASCII file has all the information about the words, characters and spaces. It has none of the information about the formatting of the document such as the text style, alignment, etc. As it lacks the formatting information, an ASCII file will be more compact than a Rich Text file, will demand less storage space and be quicker to transmit across a network. For more information about ASCII see pages 61–62.

Rich Text Format (RTF)

A file saved in RTF has all the formatting information which the ASCII file lacks, as well as the actual text. It includes all the information about styles, fonts, sizes, paragraphing and indentation.

Questions

1. Give an example of the following types of data: audio, video, animation photographic.

2. What is the purpose of a backup?

Credit

3. If you have any animated graphic files on your system, list them and examine their file sizes.

4. Explain why animated GIFs need quite a bit of memory space.

5. Pick your favourite movie. How long did it last? How much space would it take on your hard drive or DVD?

6. What is the advantage of saving files in RTF format?

Human Computer Interface

The Human Computer Interface (HCI) is the part of the computer system that people interact with. It puts the menus on the screen and handles user input.

Graphical User Interface

A Graphical User Interface (GUI) is a type of HCI in which icons and on-screen graphics are used to control a package.

Toolbar

The toolbar is a type of menu with a set of icons for tasks that are carried out frequently.

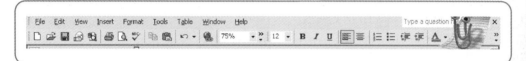

Figure 1.1 MS Word toolbar showing menu bar and Standard toolbar

The most common type of GUI is a WIMP. This stands for **W**indow, **I**con, **M**enu, **P**ointer:

◆ **Window:** an area on the screen displaying an application or a document.
◆ **Icon:** a graphic representing a file, a printer, a GPP.
◆ **Menu:** displays a range of options for the user to choose from.
◆ **Pointer:** used to select from a menu.

User friendly?

A package is said to be **user friendly** if it is easy to use. Most modern General Purpose Packages have a user friendly interface which uses windows, icons, menus and pointers.

Most GPPs provide on-line help. This includes:

◆ a help facility with an index and search feature;
◆ a text balloon which opens when you hover the pointer over an icon.

Part of the on-line help might also include an on-line tutorial. This is a part of the application that explains how to operate the package, gives examples and provides lessons. Many applications and operating systems have a 'tour' that you can take to teach you how to use its main features.

Templates

Templates are documents with the structure and much of the formatting already in place. Here is an example of some templates for a desktop publishing package. Note that they have the text and graphic frames, as well as colour schemes, fonts and sizes already in place.

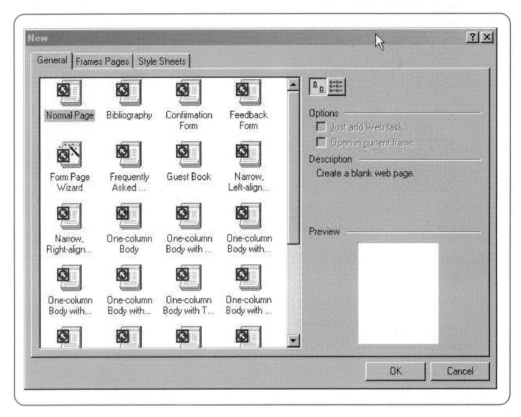

Figure 1.2 Publisher templates

The advantage of templates is that they speed up the production of a document since all the user has to do is add their own text and graphics.

Wizard

A **wizard** is a piece of software that guides you step by step through a complicated process such as installing some software, setting up a template or creating a document. The wizard uses a series of dialogue boxes and screens to step you through the process. Figure 1.3 shows a wizard for making web pages.

You can find **templates** and **wizards** in most applications.

Figure 1.3 Web page wizard

Customising the HCI

You can usually change the interface to suit yourself. For example, you can change the size of the icons, the background colour of your desktop, the speed of the pointer. Most computers let you do this by using a **control panel**.

Figure 1.4 Windows Control Panel

C **Keyboard shortcuts** are a way of getting things done quicker by pressing a key rather than going through a series of menus. A good example is this menu, which lets the user copy and paste using **control C** to copy and **control V** to paste.

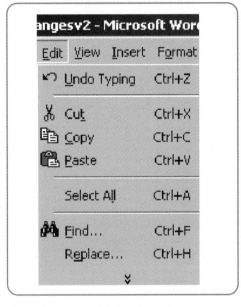

Figure 1.5 Word **Edit** drop-down menu

Questions

7. Explain the following terms: Window, Icon, Menu, Pointer.

8. How would you know if an application was not user friendly?

9. Describe the operation of a Graphical User Interface.

10. Name two facilities that will help users learn a new package.

11. What makes a toolbar such a useful feature of a GUI?

12. How can a template speed up the production of a document?

13. How can a wizard help you carry out a complicated task?

C **Credit**

14. Give two examples of customising an HCI.

15. Why do people use keyboard shortcuts?

Integrated packages

Integrated packages combine *two or more* applications in one package. An integrated package may be helpful when you have a task or series of tasks to perform which cannot be handled by one application alone. A good example is a management report drawn up for a business. Such a report would contain text created with a word processing package, columns of figures taken from a spreadsheet, lists of facts taken from a database, and illustrations and graphs.

How does it work?

The integrated package sets up links between different applications and lets them share and swap data. It lets you transfer data easily, so for example, numbers in a spreadsheet can be linked into tables on a word processor file or fields in a database.

Common HCI

An integrated package that is easy to use will have a **common HCI.** This means that each application in the integrated package is controlled by similar menus, icons and commands. If all the menus and the icons and commands are similar you don't have to learn a new set of commands or get used to a different set of menus or a new range of icons for each application.

Transferring data from one application to another also becomes straightforward. The process of transferring data will take a few commands or button clicks. A common way to move data between applications in an integrated package is to simply cut the data from one package and paste it into another.

The advantages of integrated packages

Integrated packages:

- ◆ make the transfer of data between applications easy;
- ◆ have a common HCI;
- ◆ help you set up dynamic links between files.

Integrated suite of applications

In an integrated suite, the separate applications (word processing, spreadsheets, database, and so on) can be used independently, but they share a common HCI and use common data formats. This means it is easy to transfer data between the applications, often by a simple cut and paste. Microsoft's Office suite is an example of this approach to integration.

An **advantage** of this approach is that each application will have a much wider range of features than those you find in an integrated package, where all the applications are in one package.

HOW TO PASS STANDARD GRADE COMPUTING STUDIES

A **disadvantage** is that much more computer memory is needed for the whole suite of applications.

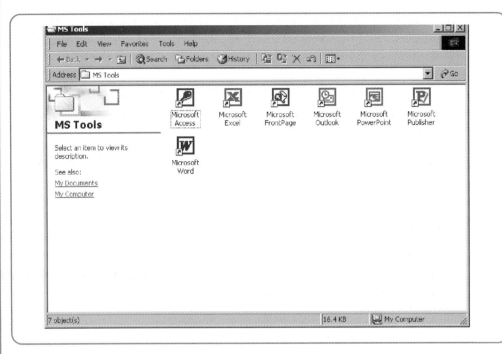

Figure 1.6 Microsoft Office integrated suite of applications

Static and dynamic linkage

An important feature of integrated software is the way in which the different applications in the integrated package are linked. There are two main ways in which this is done: **dynamic linkage** or **static linkage.**

Dynamic linkage

A link is dynamic if a change in the data in one file automatically updates the data in the file linked to it, so for example the address in a word processing document is changed as soon as the address held in a linked database file is updated.

Static linkage

If the link is static, a change in the source data does not automatically lead to the updating of the linked data. The user must interact with the package to make the link active and update the linked file. This can be done by opening the files and entering a command or choosing from a menu.

Questions

16. Your teacher is going to prepare a report for the headteacher. This will contain statistics about pupils' grades, graphs of the pattern of grades in each class and a written analysis of the performance of pupils.

    a) Why should your teacher use an integrated package?

    b) Which parts of the package will be needed for each part of the exercise?

    c) The integrated package has a WIMP based HCI. Describe how the transfer of data can be carried out.

    d) Why will your teacher find a common HCI a useful feature of the integrated package?

    e) The software offers a choice between a static and dynamic link between parts of the package. Which would you recommend be used for this task? Give your reasons.

    f) Your teacher has a choice of using an integrated suite of applications instead of an integrated package. Describe one advantage and one disadvantage in choosing the integrated suite.

Features found in all General Purpose Packages

Feature	Description
Open an application	Start the application up by selecting an icon or choosing from a menu.
Create, save or print a file	Set up a new file, save it or print it by selecting an icon or choosing from a menu.
Insert data	Enter data into a document e.g. insert a graphic into a text file.
Amend data	Change, or edit, data.
Delete	Erase, or remove, data.
Change the appearance of text	Change the size, style, font, alignment, etc.
Move data	Move data using copy and paste or cut and paste.
Headers and Footers	Reserved spaces at the top and bottom of a page – used to hold page numbers, titles, dates, authors name.
Print part of a document	Select some pages of the document to be printed.

What do you need to know about word processing packages?

Word processing packages are designed to produce text-based documents. Here is a list of standard features that you need to know about

Enter text: Entering letters, words, paragraphs – usually at the keyboard!

Word-wrap: When a word is too long to fit at the end of a line the application automatically moves the whole word onto the next line.

Alter page layout: The page can be set to be either **portrait** or **landscape**.

Set margins: You can change the widths of the margins, the non-printing areas around a page, by moving the ruler controls at the top of a page, by using the menus or by using the print preview command.

Alter the text style: You can change the appearance of the text by changing the font size and style, and by making the text **bold**, *italics*, <u>underlined</u> or coloured. This is often done for emphasis.

Alter page size: The page size can be altered in several ways. Some software sets the page length by allowing the user to set the number of lines of text per page. Others have preset sizes that the user can choose from such as A4 or US letter. The page length can also be set by inserting a page break – see below.

Standard paragraph: A standard paragraph is a paragraph of text that is already typed in, checked and saved. It can be inserted directly into a document, saving time.

Find and Replace: Using a **Find and Replace** facility allows the user to enter a word or a phrase that the package will search for, and a second word or phrase that it will replace it with. For example, you can **automatically** exchange **Stephen** for **Steven** throughout the document.

Spell Check: The spell check compares each word in a document to the list of known words, called a dictionary. It highlights any words that it does not recognise and may suggest alternatives to the user. A spell check is not foolproof and it can make two basic types of error.

It can tell you that a word is wrong when it is not – this is because the word is not in the dictionary. Common examples are proper names (like Kirkcaldy or Seonaid), abbreviations (like HCI or GUI) and foreign words.

The other type of error is when the spell check tells you that a word is okay when it is not. Common examples are using the wrong version of a word (like to/two/too or there/their/they're), misspellings that are words themselves (like missing out the **r** in **there** making 'thee') and grammar errors (like missing punctuation, capital letters, etc). So, using a spell check does not guarantee that your text is error-free!

Grammar Check: The grammar check facility checks that the text follows the rules of the English language. If a grammar rule has been broken it may offer suggestions to help improve the text.

Alter alignment: Text can be aligned on the page in four different ways – **left**, **right**, **centre** and **fully justified** (sometimes called **justified**). For each of the four, the lines of text are aligned as shown in the diagram below.

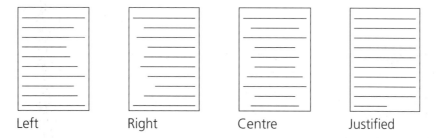

| Left | Right | Centre | Justified |

Tabulation (using tabs): Tabulation is used to align columns on text or numbers on a page. Markers are set on the ruler at the top of the page. When the tab key is pressed the cursor will jump to where the next tab marker is set. Tabs can be set for **right**, **left** and **centre** alignment. These line up columns of text in the same way as shown above, in vertical alignment. A fourth tab is a decimal tab. This is used for numbers and lines the column up on the decimal point. An example of each kind of tab is shown below.

Name	Class	Room	Score
John	2K1	J202	67.87
Frank	6G	L1	112.6
Bob	1F14	Sports hall	87
Paula	5P1	C4	79.345

| left aligned | centre aligned | right aligned | decimal tab |

Page breaks: You can force a new page at any point by selecting **insert break** from a menu.

Tables: Tables are used to organise text layout. You can set the number of rows and columns, the width of columns, the colours and borders.

Name	Subject	Room
Alastair	Computing	304
Susan	ICT	213
Lewis	Maths	112

Tables are often easier to use than tabs for simple layouts, but are not as flexible! There are many uses for tables – organising lists or linking text and graphics

Standard letters: Standard letters are letters with the same content sent to several people. The letter is stored on disk and is automatically called up and personalised by having details added such as date, names and addresses. If this is done automatically using a database, this is called a *mail merge.*

The **advantage** is that, once the document is set up, it can be reused saving time. The **disadvantages** are that any errors in the document go out to everyone on the list and that the document is rather impersonal.

Mail merge: A mail merge personalises documents such as a standard letter by inserting details such as the names and addresses from a database file or a table.

The process of setting up a mail merge is as follows:

◆ create a document using the word processing package;

◆ spell check and proof read it to ensure there are no errors;

◆ insert markers in the document where the merged data is to go;

◆ set up the link(s) between the document and the file containing the merge data;

◆ select the group of data to be used and print the desired number of copies.

It is an efficient way of producing multiple, 'personalised' copies of a document.

Scan using Optical Character Recognition: Optical Character Recognition (OCR) software can be used to enter text into your computer using a scanner. This uses a digital image of the page and produces a new word processing document that can then be edited.

The OCR software compares the shapes of each of the scanned letters to a list of known letter shapes and chooses the best match. It then adds that character to the file. The advantages of OCR are the rapid entry of text into the computer and with no need for keyboard skills All this leads to higher productivity and lower costs.

Creating a template: Creating a template in a word processing application is simple. All you have to do is set up the layout, styles, header and footer and formatting for the document and then save it into the applications Templates folder. You can then use this document shell as a starting point for future documents. For more information on templates see page 27.

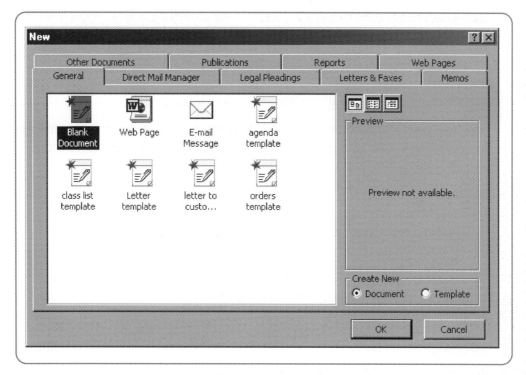

Figure 1.7 Word template options

What do you need to know about spreadsheets?

Spreadsheets are applications designed to store and process numerical data. They use a grid of cells, in rows and columns. Formulae can be used to perform calculations on the data, and various sorting and listing functions help arrange data.

Here is a list of standard spreadsheet terms and features you need to know about.

Cell: A **cell** is a location in a spreadsheet where a value can be stored. Cells are addressed using the column letter and row number so in the example, cell B3 is highlighted.

	A	B	C
1			
2			
3			
4			

Figure 1.8 Section of spreadsheet with cell B3 highlighted

Row: A **row** is a horizontal line of cells in a spreadsheet. Rows are numbered 1, 2, 3 etc.

Column: A **column** is a vertical line of cells. Each column has a letter A, B, C etc.

Value: A value is a number assigned to a cell.

Text: Cells can contain text, which includes characters, words and dates. They might be used as headings for columns of figures and totals. They are sometimes called labels.

Insert Row or Column: You can insert blank rows or columns into a spreadsheet to make room for additional numbers, formulae or headings.

Alter the width of a column: You can change how wide a column is by dragging the column boundary using the mouse and pointer or specifying column width using a dialogue box. You would use this feature when entering text or large numbers into cells. (The same can be done with row height.)

Alter cell attributes: You can change displayed characteristics of a cell. For example, you might want to change a cell so that it will show numbers to 2 decimal places. You can also display numbers as **currency**, with a £ sign, or as a **percentage**. This automatically multiplies the number by 100 and adds a % sign.

Formula: A cell can contain a calculation called a **formula**. The formula always starts with an equals sign and the result is displayed in the cell. This can involve numbers, other cells and even text. Simple formulae might use one or two mathematical symbols (+ – / *). The formula **=(A4*B4)** will multiply the contents of cells A4 and B4 together.

Complex formulae might be quite tricky! **=((A4+B4)/ (C8–16))* (D6+D7)**.

Functions: Most spreadsheets have a set of standard mathematical functions. You are required to know and be able to use **four** simple functions: SUM, AVERAGE, MIN and MAX.

Function	Description of effect
=SUM(C4:C42)	Adds the values in the cells in the range C4 to C42
=AVERAGE(A1:A12)	Calculates the average of all the cells in the range A1 to A12
=MIN(A4:G4)	Calculates the smallest number in the range A4 to G4
=MAX(F3:F34)	Calculates the largest number in the range F3 to F34

At Credit, you are also expected to be able to use the IF function. This function is used to allow choices to be made. It looks something like this:

= IF (B4 >= 21,'Pass', 'Fail')

This translates as:

If the contents of cell **B4** are greater than or equal to **21**

then display the word '**Pass**'

otherwise display the word '**Fail**'.

The first part of the bracket **B4>=21** is the **condition**. The second part of the bracket **'Pass'** is what is shown if the condition is **true** and the last part **'Fail'** is what is displayed if the condition is **false**. The output could be text, numbers or even another formula!

Replication: Quite often, you will want to carry out the same calculation a number of times in a spreadsheet. Instead of typing in the same formula over and over again, you can get the spreadsheets program to copy a formula across a row or down a column. This is sometimes called **fill down** or **fill right**.

Here you type in your formula, select the cells that you want the formula to be in and then fill the formula down or right using the menus.

	A	B	C
1	Hours worked	Rate	Pay
2	12	4.12	=A2*B2
3	23	5.50	
4	14	13.80	
5	16	24.50	

When a formula is replicated it will change automatically to match its new position. Using the example above, when the formula is copied from C2 into C3 and the other cells below, the new formula in **C5** will be **=A5*B5**. You will learn more about this later, in the section about relative and absolute references.

Automatic and manual calculation: You can control when the spreadsheet performs calculations. When entering data with the automatic calculation facility on, the spreadsheet will **automatically recalculate** all the formulae if any changes are made to the data. With **manual** calculation the formulae will not be calculated until the user enters a command. This allows many numbers to be changed before any recalculation is done.

Cell protection: If you want to protect the contents of a cell or set of cells from being changed or deleted, you can apply cell protection. This would usually apply to the labels or the formulae that you have carefully worked out and don't want to have to do all over again! The process of applying cell protection is also know as locking the cell.

Charting: It's often very useful to be able to show data on a graph, and most spreadsheet applications allow you to create a wide range of charts and graphs.

This makes it easy to see what they mean at a glance. You make a chart by selecting the area of the spreadsheet that contains the data to be charted. Then you use the menus, buttons or wizard to make your chart.

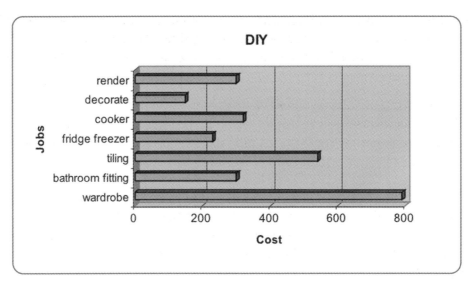

Figure 1.9 Excel chart

Fully labelled chart

A fully labelled chart has the following set of text labels:

◆ **key** for the chart (called a label for the chart series);

◆ **title** for each individual chart;

◆ label for each of the X and Y **axes**;

◆ label for each **item** on a chart showing its relation to the data.

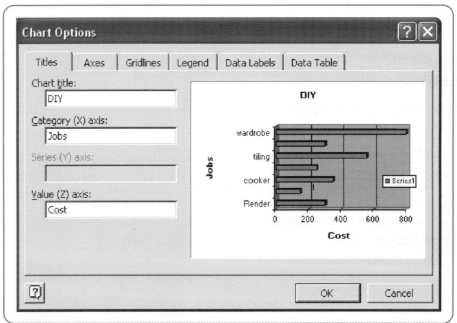

Figure 1.10 Excel chart with **Chart Options** window

Relative and absolute referencing: When formulae or functions are replicated, the cells they refer to are either **relative** or **absolute**. An **absolute** reference is used when the formula always needs to refer to a particular cell for all calculations. We don't want this cell to change when the formula is copied.

In a wages spreadsheet, column B might contain the number of hours worked, column C might contain the hourly rate at which the worker is paid and cell F1 contains the bonus paid to every worker before the Summer holiday. The formula

=B2*C2+F1 is used in cell **D2**.

If we copy the formula onto another row, all the row references will change automatically. We want to change the row references for the number of hours worked and the hourly rate, but we don't want to change the bonus, so we need to fix the bonus to one cell. We can do this by changing the reference for F1 to an **absolute** reference using dollar signs.

=B2 * C2 + F1

Copy this down the column and the first two **relative** references will change but the third reference will remain the same, as it is **absolute**. In cell D14 the formula will be:

D2				=B2*C2+F1	
	A	B	C	D	E	F
		Number of hours worked	Hourly rate	Total pay	Summer bonus	£250
1						
2	T Roberts	35	8.0	£530		
3	J Swinson	34	7.6	£258		
4	P Cuthbert	38	7.6	£289		
5	A Wilson	39	9.2	£359		
6						

=B14 * C14 + F1

Questions

17. Explain the following terms:
    Word-wrap
    Standard paragraph   Grammar check
    Text style   Table
    Find and replace   Page break

Credit

    Standard letter
    Mail merge

Questions

18. Explain the following terms:
    Row
    Column
    Cell
    Formula
    SUM function
    Automatic calculation
    Simple charting
    Complex formula
    AVERAGE function
    MINIMUM function
    MAXIMUM function
    Replicate
    Cell attributes
    Cell protection

C **Credit**

19. Write out the syntax of a formula using the IF function.

20. Explain the difference between a relative reference and an absolute reference.

What do you need to know about databases?

A **database** is an organised list of information. A database application is a program, like FileMaker Pro or Microsoft Access, designed to **store**, **search** and **sort** data. You should be familiar with these features of databases.

File (datafile): Data is stored in **files**, or **datafiles**, and manipulated by a database program. Files are made up of sets of records.

Record: A **record** contains all the information about one item in the file. For example, a car dealership would have a database with files for all the cars for sale. Each car would have a unique record, made up of a set of fields, such as make and model, colour, engine size and registration number.

Field: A field holds **single** item of data in the database, such as a field for the registration number of a car.

Add records: A new record is added to the file and relevant data entered into the fields of that record.

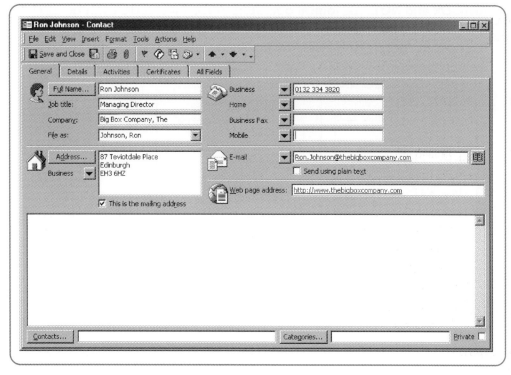

Figure 1.11 Fields and records in a database

Create fields: To define, or set up, new fields in a record you need to plan **exactly** what information you want to hold on your **data subjects**. You may need to decide on the field names, field types and field sizes.

Field types: There are many types of field. You **need** to know about **five** types:

◆ *numeric* fields to hold numbers, e.g. exam marks

◆ *text* fields to hold words e.g. forenames of pupils

◆ *graphic* fields to hold images e.g. photographs

◆ *date* fields to hold dates, e.g. date of birth

◆ *time* fields to hold times, e.g. start time of exam

Search on one field: An essential part of a database is the ability to search specific fields and records. A search is also called **query** or a **find**. A **simple** search on the database file involves searching on one field only, e.g. search for those records where the *first_name* field = 'Jack'.

Search on more than one field: A complex search is based on two or more fields, e.g. search for those records where the *first_name* field = 'Jean' AND the *second_name* field = 'Brown'.

AND, OR and NOT: The **logical operators AND, OR** and **NOT can be** used in searches. The diagrams below explain how they are used. The two groups in the diagrams are 'people with blue eyes' and 'males'. The shaded areas correspond to the results of the search.

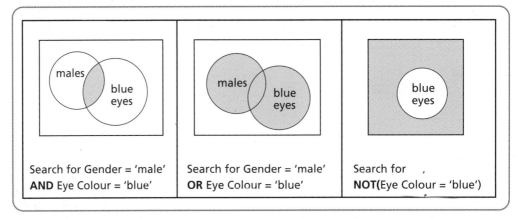

Figure 1.12 Venn diagrams to show AND, OR and NOT searches

Sort on one field: You can arrange, or **sort**, the records into order based on the contents of one field. A common arrangement would involve sorting names alphabetically, which you might describe as 'sort on the *Second_name* field in **ascending** order' (from 'a' to 'z').

Sort on more than one field: A **complex sort**, where two or more fields are used to arrange the data e.g. sort class file on *grade* field and *surname* field, both in ascending order. This will sort the records so that the grades are in order, with all those with grade 1 followed by grade 2 etc, and each of these groups is sorted into alphabetical order of surname.

Grade	Surname
1	Carrick
1	Dorward
1	Howard
1	Thomson
2	Campbell
2	McCulloch
2	Robertson
2	Shearer

Alter a record format: It may be necessary to alter a record format by changing the **structure** of a record in a database. This could be done by:

◆ changing the **number** of fields in the record by adding or deleting one of them;

◆ changing the **length** of a field, enabling it to hold more characters;

◆ changing the **type** of field from e.g. numeric to text.

Searches on a CD-ROM: CD-ROMs are often used to hold a great deal of information, for example CD-based encyclopedias such as Encarta. Such an encyclopedia will hold text, graphics, audio and video clips.

Simple search: The encyclopedia will have a **search engine** that will let you search for things with simple text entry in search box. This would give you thousands of 'castle' entries, most of them you would not want.

Figure 1.13 Simple search term in a search engine.

Complex search: Sometimes it is not so easy to find what you want. You may have to carry out a **complex search,** where you set up **conditions** that the search has to meet.

Figure 1.14 Complex search terms in a search engine.

Using conditions can make your search more accurate. The more conditions you put into your search, the more refined it will be and the more accurate as the conditions include exactly what you want and exclude things you do not.

Figure 1.15 Complex search terms in a search engine.

For more information on searching on the Internet see the Communications and Networks chapter on page 48.

Computed field: A computed field, sometimes called a *calculated* field, is one that contains a formula using one or more other fields in the record or file. Examples of this might be a Grade field that uses the marks field to calculate the grade awarded to the candidate.

Keyword: A keyword field contains words, phrases or numbers to make searching easier, so a keyword field in a films database might contain words like 'comedy',

C

'horror' to allow faster searching. The exam board will use your Candidate Number as a keyword.

Alter Screen Input Format: Altering the Screen Input Format changes the arrangement of the data fields and their field names in a data entry form as it is displayed on screen.

Alter Output Format: In the same way as you can change the input format, you can also change the arrangement of fields and records as they are displayed and/or printed out. For example you might want four or five fields in a *columnar report* of exam results!

Questions ?

21. Explain these terms:
    File
    Record
    Field
    Alter record format
    Give an example of:
    A **Search, query or find** on **one field**
    A **Sort** on **one field**
    A **Search** on **more than one field**
    A **Sort** on **more than one field**

C **Credit**
    Explain these terms:
    Keyword
    Altering the screen output format
    Altering the screen input format

What do you need to know about graphics?

Graphics packages are used to create and edit pictures and images. Some word processing packages can be used to create simple graphics and carry out simple editing, capabilities, but full graphics packages have a very wide selection of drawing and editing options. Because they deal with images instead of text or numbers, graphics packages often need a lot of computer memory.

Draw graphic: Graphics are pictures produced by computer. They can be produced in a **drawing** package (**vector** graphics) or a **painting** package (**bitmapped** graphics).

Enter text: Text is used to label and explain graphics.

Common tools: Graphics packages usually have a GUI to allow the user to select the drawing tools they want using icons. These **tools** will include **line** tools, tools for **circles/ovals**, **rectangle** tools and other shapes. They may also include tools to change the way the shape looks on screen or to change its attributes, like fill colour and line thickness.

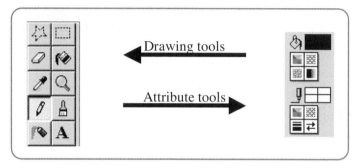

Figure 1.16 Drawing tools and Attribute tools in a graphics package

Alter tool attributes: You can change the properties of a tool or object to change the thickness, colour or pattern of a drawing line or paintbrush.

Scale graphic: You can change the dimensions of a graphic by altering its height or width.

Rotate graphic: You can turn a graphic around to view it from another angle by dragging the graphic using the mouse and cursor, or by entering the number of degrees through which the graphic will turn.

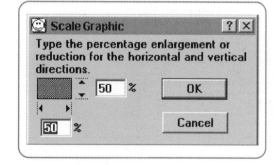

Figure 1.17 **Scale Graphics** dialog box

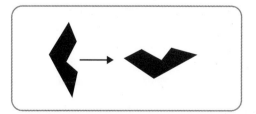

Figure 1.18 Geometric shape undergoing rotation

Cropping a graphic: If an image is the wrong size, or if you only want a part of a picture, you cut out an area of a graphic by cropping it. Here you see a picture of a mountain being cropped – the dotted line shows the area to be retained.

Figure 1.19 Image of mountain being cropped in Photoshop.

Scanning a graphic: Scanning a graphic allows you to capture a picture for use on the computer. To do this effectively you have to choose:

◆ the **resolution**, number of pixels per inch, of the scan;

◆ the **colour depth**, number of colours each pixel can have;

◆ the **type** of file the graphic is saved as – bitmap, jpeg or gif.

Editing the scanned graphic: Once you have scanned an image, it is saved in digital format, so you can edit it in the same way as any graphic created with a graphics package. The range of editing features available to you depends on the software you use. Common editing features are crop; rotate; scale; select colour; layer onto other graphic objects; zoom in or out; add special effects.

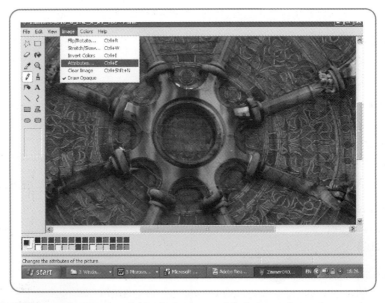

Figure 1.20 Image within Paintbox with **Image** drop-down menu showing.

Questions ?

22. Explain these terms:
   Tool attributes
   Scale graphic
   Rotate graphic

Credit
   Crop graphic
   Scan graphic
   Edit graphic

What do you need to know about desktop publishing?

Desktop publishing (DTP) applications are designed to produce documents that combine text and graphics with great precision such as newsletters, magazines, pamphlets, company reports, brochures and so on.

DTP packages often use wizards and templates to guide you through the process of creating a document with mixed text and graphics.

Wizards: A **wizard** is a small program, built into the package, that will help you produce documents by taking you through steps necessary to carry out the more complex tasks.

Templates: Most DTP packages have a whole range of **templates** for you to choose from. Templates help you because they are documents with most of the formatting and layout already set up e.g. the fonts, sizes, text and graphic frames and colours.

Importing graphics files: DTP packages enable you to **import** graphics from clip art, photographs, the Internet or graphics you have created using a graphics package. After a graphic has been imported you may have to *scale* it to fit your document. For more about scaling graphics see the Graphics section.

Importing text: DTP packages enable you to set up a *text frame* and bring in your text from a word processing document. This is similar to importing a graphic.

Change layout: You can change the layout of your document by altering the position of text frames, and graphic objects using the precise control which comes with desktop publishing applications.

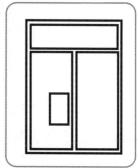

Figure 1.21 Outline page with text frames and graphic objects.

c **Text wrap around graphics**: This facility enables you to let your text flow around a graphic.

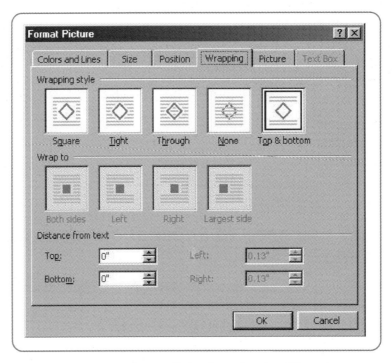

Figure 1.22 Format Picture dialog box showing Wrapping options.

This lets you position your graphic for maximum effect by embedding it in the text.

This is an example of text that has been tightly wrapped around a picture. Here the text is put as close to the picture as is possible without obscuring the graphic.

Figure 1.23 Small image with text wrapped around it.

What do you need to know about presentation and multimedia?

Presentation and multimedia packages use **wizards** and **templates,** as described above, to guide you through the process of creating a multimedia presentation. A multimedia presentation will normally be a series of linked slides containing text, graphics, audio and even video materials.

Linear linkage of slides: Most presentation packages link slides together automatically so that they follow one after another. Moving between slides is simply a matter of a mouse click or a tap on the return key.

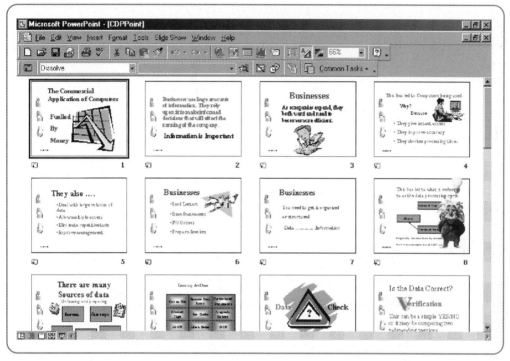

Figure 1.24 PowerPoint presentation with slide show displayed.

Using hyperlinks: Hyperlinks can be used to link slides together, allowing you to jump from one slide to another. This is often used to provide different routes through your slides. The screenshot here shows a hyperlink being set to jump to slide 8 (on audio data).

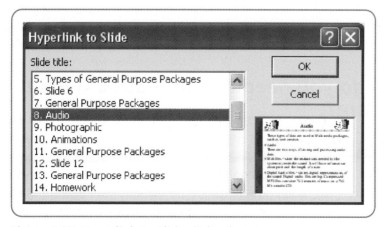

Figure 1.25 Hyperlink to Slide dialog box.

GENERAL PURPOSE PACKAGES

HOW TO PASS STANDARD GRADE COMPUTING STUDIES

Add audio to your multimedia document: You can add interest to a multimedia document by attaching an audio file to a slide.

Add video: Adding a video clip can really bring a presentation alive and keep an audience's attention. The process involved is usually straightforward and consists of selecting a file containing a video clip from a folder.

Assembling the elements of a presentation: Once you have gathered the graphics, audio, video and text materials for your presentation you can assemble them into a series of slides. You can rehearse the presentation and make changes to the order the slides are shown in.

Capturing audio: Sounds can be captured by recording tracks from an audio CD, a MIDI keyboard, using a microphone or downloading from the Internet. Linking your sound files to a slide is then straightforward.

Capturing images: Images can be captured using a digital camera, a scanner or by downloading an image from the Internet. These can then be added to your presentation.

Questions ?

23. Explain these terms:
    Template
    Slides with linear links
    Import graphic

C **Credit**
    Import text
    Change layout
    Text wrap around graphics

What do you need to know about web page software?

Web page software is used to create pages for websites. All web page software allows you to enter both text and graphics (clip art or photos) so that they can be viewed using a web browser. The simplest method to produce web pages is to create a page using a word processing package and then saving the files as **.htm** files. However there are a number of excellent packages that offer many more features to the budding web designer.

Using a wizard or a template: Web page applications have wizards or templates already set up to get you off to a good start.

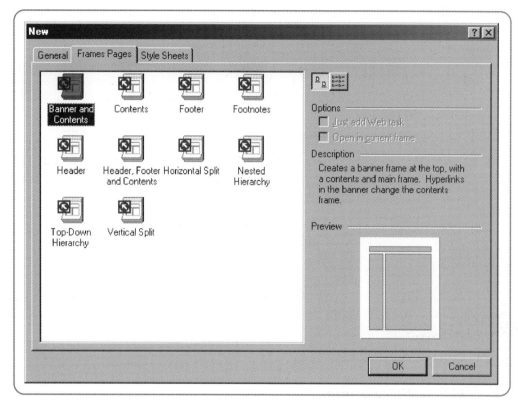

Figure 1.26 Templates for frame pages used in MS FrontPage.

Using hyperlinks: Hyperlinks are used to link, or move, from one web page to another. You link your web pages by setting up hyperlinks. Setting up a hyperlink is quite straightforward. Simply choose the section that you want to link from and then insert a hyperlink using the menus. The package will then ask you to browse and point to the page you want to link to. One web page can have many hyperlinks on it. You can choose a range of objects to link you to the next page, such as a piece of text or a graphic as a link.

Text link	Graphic link
Click here to open the presentation	Click on the graphic to open the presentation

Use hyperlinks to help users find their way around your website: If your website is complex it can be easy for users to get lost. It is necessary to help the user find their way around the website by giving them a choice of well-marked routes through your material. This can be done by using hyperlinks that can be organised into menus, making it easier for the user to get to key menus and to the homepage.

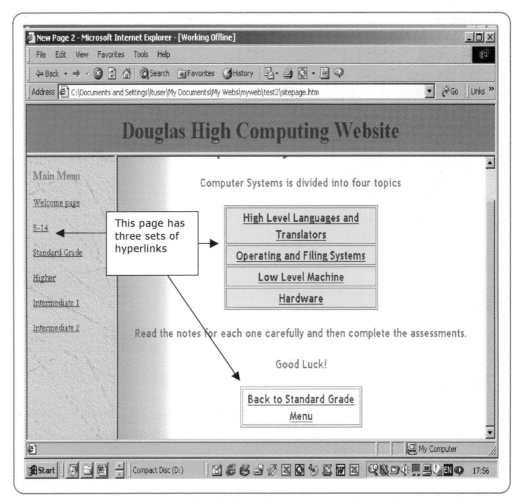

Figure 1.28 Website showing position of sets of hyperlinks.

Adding a hotspot: A hotspot is a user-defined area on a web page or multimedia document that is linked to an **event**. An event might be an action like revealing a graphic, opening up a text frame or jumping to another part of the document. Events can be set to trigger when the user does something, like clicking the mouse button or even just moving the cursor over an area containing a hotspot.

Adding tables: Tables are an important part of the structure of a web page. They are often used to hold graphics and their linked text together as well as for holding columns of numbers, lists of names, addresses and even hyperlinks.

C ## A table holding a graphic and text together

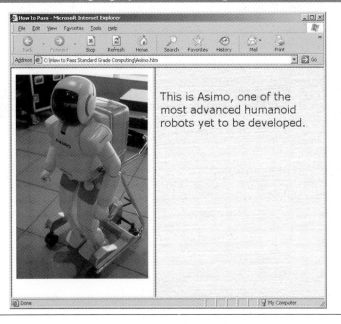

This is Asimo, one of the most advanced humanoid robots yet to be developed.

Questions

You are designing a website or multimedia presentation on your favourite sport.

24. What would you use to link your pages together?

25. Why you might want to link your slides or pages in a more complex way?

C **Credit**

26. What would tables add to your web page?

27. What would hotspots add to your web page?

What do you need to know about expert systems?

An expert system is a programme which makes decisions or solves problems by using knowledge and rules defined by experts in a particular subject area.

How are expert systems set up?

A group of experts in a subject set down all the facts and rules that apply to the system. These rules and facts are checked and then entered into an expert system. The expert system acts like an intelligent database that asks the user questions about the problem and matches the answers to facts that it already knows. It then gives the user advice on what to do next.

Where are expert systems used?

There are many applications for expert systems. Some of the areas where expert systems have been successfully applied include:

◆ Medical systems like MYCIN and PUFF to help diagnose and treat illnesses.

◆ Geology and oil exploration has been supported by software like PROSPECTOR.

◆ Banking, insurance and the stock market have benefited from the detailed analysis provided by this kind of software.

◆ Systems like LIMEX have been helping Egyptian farmers plan for the future.

◆ Car mechanics use diagnostic systems to track engine faults quickly.

◆ Computer engineers use expert systems to help set up and test networks.

Advantages of expert systems

◆ They hold all the knowledge of an expert in a software application. All a user has to do is ask the computer a question and the system will provide an expert answer.

◆ They support people when they have to make decisions by providing expert advice when no human expert is available, like up a mountain!

◆ The knowledge is not lost if the experts are ill or die.

◆ The system does not forget or miss a detail.

◆ The expert system, being a program, can be duplicated and given to many more people than would normally be able to consult a human expert.

◆ They can teach people about a subject by giving the answers to questions then giving the reasons for the answers.

Questions

28. What is the purpose of an expert system?

29. How is an expert system set up?

30. Give three examples of how an expert system is used.

Credit

31. Give three advantages of an expert system.

Selecting a package for a task

You should now be able to select the correct package for any task that is given to you. Answer these questions.

32. Which package would you use to produce:

   a) a letter to the parents of all the pupils in the first year?

   b) a poster for the school disco?

   c) a leaflet on countryside walks near your school?

   d) a slide show on the subject of your school trip to France?

   e) a file with the names and addresses of your school friends?

   f) a document with the results of the school basketball competition?

   g) a multimedia training package to help people use the school computer system?

   h) a program to help people invest their savings?

Social, legal and economic implications

What are the implications of the increased use of GPPs?

In considering the increased use of GPPs, we need to ask what implications or effects there are on individuals, society and businesses as a result of these changes.

Jobs

The use of GPPs and computers has a range of effects on peoples' jobs. New jobs are often created, as people have to be employed to set up and maintain the hardware and software systems. Many jobs may be lost, as the work of many can now be done more effectively by fewer people.

Training

For the people using the systems the main implication is that there is a great need for training. Every time a new computer system or a new application is installed staff need to be trained. As a result of the training the staff may be paid more, as they are more highly skilled.

Working conditions

Offices have to be designed to cope with computers. Health and safety is important. Computer desks must be designed properly, adjustable chairs need to be installed as does good ventilation and lighting.

Increased paper?

People once thought that using computers would mean the end of documents being produced on paper and that everything would be held electronically on computer. Although everything is held electronically, we still produce lots of documents on paper. At work and at home people produce lots of printouts using their computer systems.

Costs

When installing a computer system there are **four** main types of costs involved:

- initial costs;
- replacement costs;
- running costs;
- staff costs.

Initial costs are those that have to be met when a computerised system is set up. These include:

- purchasing and installing the hardware and the applications;
- equipping the computer work areas with appropriate furniture, like desks and adjustable chairs;
- staff training costs.

The **replacement cost** of monitors, keyboards, hard drives and software will have to be considered. The software for a business machine can run to several hundred pounds per computer.

Running costs are made up of many things and include maintenance costs, consumables (like disks, tapes, printer paper and toner) and other operational overheads such as telephone and data transmission bills.

Staff costs are the costs incurred in employing and training staff to run and use the computer systems. Staff costs can include:

- paying for the systems analyst;
- paying for the engineers who install the cabling and the hardware;
- paying for the software experts who install the software;
- employing experts to train the staff (this can represent a steep initial staff cost);
- staff to use the system on a daily basis.

Security and privacy

There is a need to protect people's privacy regarding information held about them on computer systems. People have the **right of access to data** that is held about them on computer systems. There are **exceptions** to this right to see data. For example, you have not right of access if the data is held by the Police, security forces or the Inland Revenue.

Data security

Once it is stored in the computer system the data must be protected against accidental loss or damage. This can be done by making sure that a proper system of **multiple backup copies** is in place and that the copies are regularly updated. Such backup copies should be securely stored in different locations e.g. in safes in different offices.

Data Protection Act

The Data Protection Act gives the conditions for keeping data and for making it available. There are **three** groups of people named in the Act. These are **data subjects**, **data users** and **data controllers**.

Data subjects

In the Act individuals to whom data relates are known as **data subjects.** Data subjects have the following **rights**:

◆ to know if data is held about them on a computer system and to have a copy and a description of that data;

◆ to know the purposes for which the data is being processed and who is going to receive the data;

◆ to inspect such data and to have it changed if they think it is inaccurate;

◆ to ask for compensation if data is inaccurate or if an unauthorised person has been given access to it;

◆ to prevent processing of data likely to cause damage or distress;

◆ to be sure that decisions made about them are not made only on the basis of automatic processing such as psychometric testing for jobs.

For all of these, data subjects can be charged a single administration fee. A data subject can apply to the courts to block the processing of data or to correct, erase or destroy it.

Data user

A data user is an individual within an organisation who makes use of personal data. The **data user** must keep to the following **Data Protection Principles**. All personal data should be:

◆ processed only if the consent of the individual is given, if it is part of a legal contract, if it is essential to a business transaction or the carrying out of public duties;

◆ held for the specified purposes described in the Register entry;

◆ accurate and where necessary be kept up to date;

◆ relevant and not excessive in relation to the purpose for which they are held;

◆ adequate for the purpose specified;

◆ processed in accordance with the rights of the data subject;

37

- ◆ surrounded by proper security, like passwords and/or encryption;
- ◆ transferred only to countries outside of the EU that have adequate security measures as defined in the Act.

Data controller

The **data controller** is defined as the person, business or organisation who controls the collection and use of personal data. The **data controller** must:

- ◆ register with the **Data Protection Commissioner**;
- ◆ apply for permission to keep personal data on computers;
- ◆ state what data they want to keep, its purpose and who has access to it.

Data Protection Register

The Data Protection Register holds the details about who holds information on members of the public on computer systems. The Data Protection Register can be found in central libraries.

Data Protection Commissioner

If anyone has a problem accessing data or has a complaint about the accuracy of data, they can contact the office of the **Data Protection Registrar,** who oversees the administration of the Act.

Copyright, Designs and Patents Act

The Copyright, Designs and Patents Act deals with the problem of computer software, which now is protected by law for fifty years after the death of the author of the software. It makes it illegal to:

- ◆ make unauthorised (pirate) copies of software;
- ◆ run pirate software;
- ◆ transmit software over telecommunications links and copy it;
- ◆ run multiple copies of software if only one copy was purchased;
- ◆ give, lend or sell copies of bought software unless license to do so is granted.

Hackers and hacking

Hackers are people who try to break into computer systems and steal or corrupt data. The main defence against hacking is to control access to computer systems using a system of **IDs** and **passwords**. Other techniques might include encryption of sensitive data or more secure hardware, like dedicated network cables. Most hackers gain access by the simple method of guessing a password or finding a way in that has no password.

Computer Misuse Act

The Computer Misuse Act is designed to make hacking into a computer system illegal and subject to penalties. This act makes it an offence to **gain unauthorised**

C **access** to a computer system or to make **unauthorised modifications** to computer materials. Modifying computer material is defined by the Act as:

◆ interfering with a system so that it doesn't run properly;

◆ making changes to the system to prevent others accessing the system;

◆ making changes to the software or data;

Penalties of up to five years imprisonment and fines apply.

Questions

33. Why do people need to be retrained when a new computer system is introduced to a workplace?

34. Do people have the right to see all information held about them on a computer system?

35. Give an example of an initial cost.

36. Give an example of a replacement cost.

37. Give an example of a running cost.

38. Give an example of a staff cost.

39. Does the use of computer systems lead to a decrease in the amount of paper being used?

40. What is the main way to control access to a computer system?

41. What do we call someone who accesses a computer system without authorisation?

Credit

42. Describe each of the following: data subject, data controller, data user.

43. List three principles of the Data Protection Act which a data user must keep to.

44. What is 'modifying computer materials' defined as in the Computer Misuse Act?

45. List three activities made illegal by the Copyright Designs and Patents Act.

Chapter 2

COMMUNICATIONS AND NETWORKS

Key Words

★ **types of network**
★ **security**
★ **Internet**
★ **web pages**

★ **transmission media**
★ **electronic communication**
★ **e-mail**

Network

A **network** comprises two or more computers linked together. They can be linked using cables or wireless connections. Networks can be expensive to set up and there are security issues around how to control access to data, but there are many advantages.

The **advantages** of networks are that users can:

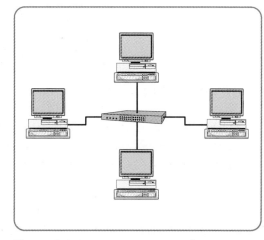

Figure 2.1 A computer network.

- ◆ **share peripherals** such as hard drives and printers;
- ◆ **share data** and programs;
- ◆ work on **shared projects**;
- ◆ communicate by sending **emails**;
- ◆ **backup** data more effectively;
- ◆ control **security** more effectively.

Local Area Network

A **Local Area Network (LAN)** is a small network on a single room, building or site. Examples are a school network, a network in an office or a home network for game playing. They usually use the same type of cabling and networking software.

Wide Area Network

A **Wide Area Network** (**WAN**) is physically larger than a LAN. It can link computers across towns, countries and around the world. They often use a variety of methods of connection to transmit information, such as physical cables, the telephone network, microwave transmitters and even satellites! They tend to be slower and more prone to errors than LANs, but they can allow us to work anywhere on the planet.

Transmission media

A **transmission medium** is the type of connection used to join computers together. These can be physical cables or wireless connections. The table below compares some of the different types of transmission media.

Name	Description
Twisted pair	This cable consists of two copper wires twisted around each other. It is widely used because it is cheap and capable of transmitting data quickly, at speeds of 100 megabits per second.
Coaxial	This cabling is not so commonly used as twisted pair as it is more expensive. It has a protective shield to prevent interference and is used in situations where interference can corrupt data.
Fibre-optic	Fibre-optic cable is made up of fine strands of glass that transmit data as pulses of light. Fibre-optic cable transmits at very high speeds. It also doesn't lose data because of interference and is very secure. It is very expensive to install.

Wireless networking

Wireless networks use radio waves, microwaves or infrared light to transmit data. All you need is a transmitter/receiver in every machine and a central device, such as a wireless router, to pass their data around the network. Any modern computer can be fitted with a wireless network card, sometimes by just plugging it into the USB slot.

They are easy to install, as there is no need for cables. You can move around when you work without trailing wires. They have reasonably fast transmission speeds, although they are slower than physical cables. The main problem is that they are vulnerable to hackers, who can just 'tap in' to your signal. You need to take care when setting up network security if you don't want others to access your files or use your Internet connection.

Network Interface Card

A **Network Interface Card** (**NIC**) is needed for all devices connected to a LAN, including peripherals like printers. The NIC sends the data in a format that the network understands. It also recognises data addressed to your computer, captures it and sends it on to the processor.

C Client/server network

Most networks in offices and businesses are **client/server networks.** A **client** is a **workstation** on the network. A **server** is a powerful computer with a fast processor and large memory capacity. A server controls the **resources** on the network that are available for the client workstations to use.

A network can have a range of servers:

◆ **Print** server, controlling printing resources;

◆ **File** server, controlling access to files;

◆ **Application** server, controlling access to application packages;

◆ **Mail** server, storing and passing e-mail;

◆ **Web** server, controlling access to the Internet.

Multi-access

In multi-access networks, many users can share one computer's resources at the same time. These computers are usually very powerful in large networks. Multi-access computers are used by large businesses and organisations such as banks and mail-order companies, although you *could* make your own computer multi-access in a home LAN!

Terminals

Large multi-access systems are often accessed using **terminals** connected to a mainframe or a server. Terminals have very little, if any, processing power or memory of their own. They rely upon the processing power and memory on the central powerful computer system.

Security on networks

Security measures are needed to prevent data being copied, changed or deleted.

Physical security

To protect against unauthorised access, you can use **physical** security measures such as:

◆ security locks on the doors and windows of computer rooms;

◆ locks on workstations themselves;

◆ no removable backing storage, such as floppy drives.

System security

You can use other techniques to protect data on your network. Common techniques are:

◆ unique **network IDs** to identify users;

◆ **network passwords** to prove users are who they say;

◆ **encryption** to make data unreadable to those who cannot unlock the code;

- **password protection** for individual files if they contain sensitive data;
- multi-level **access rights**, where some people only get partial access;
- **biometric systems**, like fingerprint or retinal scanners.

Questions

1. List two advantages of a LAN.

2. Describe one advantage and one disadvantage of wireless networks.

3. What is a WAN?

4. Describe three physical and three system security methods.

Credit

5. Why is a NIC card needed?

6. What is a multi-access computer?

7. Give an example of a server on a network.

Electronic communication

Text messaging

Text messaging (or **instant messaging**) is one of the most flexible methods of modern communication. Mobile phones, or PCs, are used to send short messages, text or picture, to other users. These messages can be sent directly to pagers, mobile phones and palmtop computers with mobile phone connections (smartphones). They can also be sent to message servers that act in the same way as e-mail servers.

Electronic-mail (e-mail)

You can send e-mail across a LAN, a WAN or the Internet. E-mail enables us to communicate, instantly and cheaply, with people right around the world. Advantages of e-mail include:

- speed of delivery compared with surface mail;
- low cost compared with surface mail;
- you can sent attachments, documents or pictures, around the world;
- ability to check mail from any network workstation or Internet connection;
- security: mail is protected by IDs and passwords;

◆ ability to send multiple copies of mail at the one time;

◆ ability to store and organise messages.

There are a number of problems with the growing use of e-mail, and disadvantages of e-mail include:

◆ e-mail attachments can contain **viruses**;

◆ **junk mail** arrives by e-mail;

◆ **disk space** is wasted by people who do not delete e-mail;

◆ it is difficult to monitor the **content** of attachments.

File transfer using e-mail attachments

Attaching a file to an e-mail message is a simple and efficient way to send someone a copy of a file. The process of attaching a file is straightforward and is usually just a mouse click to select the file for transfer.

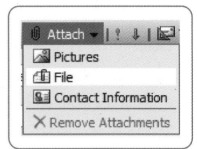

Figure 2.2 Attach menu in e-mail application

E-mail providers put **limits** the size and number of files that can be attached to e-mails up to a maximum of about 10 Mb per message. Attachments are sometimes used to send viruses, so unexpected attachments must be treated with care.

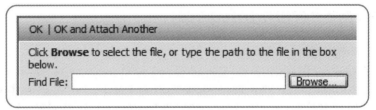

Figure 2.3 Attach/find file dialog box

Netiquette

Netiquette is a code of conduct, or set of rules, to guide behaviour when using e-mail or a network. A netiquette code could contain rules like:

Do not send spam, repeat e-mails that annoy and clog up the system.

Be polite, say 'please' and 'thanks' when sending messages.

Do not use capital letters, it is considered to be SHOUTING.

Do not start arguments (flame wars) using e-mail.

Do not send chain messages.

Discussion points: Are these good rules? What are the reasons for having these rules?

The Internet

The Internet is a global network of networks. It uses telecommunications equipment to connect computers and networks across the world. The Internet is vast, it contains almost everything you might want, and quite a lot of stuff you really want to avoid. It is like walking into the world library of everything! However, you need to verify your sources, as a lot of the data on the Internet is not completely accurate. Despite these problems, many businesses rely on the Internet for their survival. Many people do most of their shopping online or book the holidays for the summer.

Web pages

The graphical part of the Internet, the **World Wide Web**, carries most of the traffic on the Internet. It is made up of **multimedia web pages** that are stored on computers across the world. Web pages hold text, sounds, graphics, animations, and videos. These are linked together by **hyperlinks.**

Movie Clips

A hyperlink appears either as underlined text such as Computing Revision or as a graphic, like the one shown here. Clicking on a hyperlink instructs the browser to fetch a web page and display it.

Figure 2.4 Small hyperlink-style graphic

Creating a web page

You can create a web page using a word processing package and saving it as a web page. To create a really professional looking page you need to use a *web page authoring* package. Read the GPP chapter for more detail. The language that the web page is written in is called **HTML (HyperText Markup Language)**. HTML is a page description language which uses tags or commands to set up the headings, colours, graphics and text that make up a web page. The computer reads the information about how the page should look and draws it on the screen.

Connecting to the Internet

One way to access the Internet is to use an **Internet-ready computer system**.

A computer system is **Internet-ready** when it has a telecommunications link (using a **modem** and either **broadband** or **dial-up** connections), **browser** software and a link to an **Internet Service Provider** (ISP).

A **modem** (**mo**dulator/**dem**odulator) changes digital data signals into sound so that it can be sent down a phone line. It also receives sound and demodulates it, changing it back from sound to data. For the higher bandwidth connections you may need a cable modem.

A dial-up connection is a connection to the Internet that uses an ordinary phone line and a modem to dial up and connect a computer to the Internet. It has a bandwidth (or speed) of 56 kilobits per second (kbps). That means that a 70 kilobyte file, like a small graphic, will take 10 seconds to download on an ordinary phone line (A kilobyte is 8 kilobits, so a 70 kilobyte file is 560 kilobits, so the time taken is 560 kilobits divided by 56 kilobits per second = 10 seconds. Take care not to mix up bits and bytes!).

A broadband connection is a high-speed telecommunications link that works 10+ times faster than a dial-up connection. The standard bandwidths for this type of connection are from 0.5 megabits per second (mbps) to 2 mbps.

There are other types of connection but they are really expensive and only suitable for businesses! Try looking up *ISDN*, *ASDL*, and *leased lines* on your favourite search engine.

A **browser** is a program that helps you navigate the **World Wide Web**, move between and look at web pages. You can enter the address of the page you want to go to or you can click on a **hyperlink**.

Figure 2.5 Internet Explorer showing Google toolbar with search term: computer network LAN.

A browser can remember where pages are if the address is added to the **Favourites** list on the browser. This makes it easy to view websites you use often.

A computer is **online** when it is connected and ready to send and receive data. It is offline when it is not connected to the network. When you connect to your ISP, you go online.

Internet Service Providers (ISPs)

An Internet Service Provider (ISP) provides users with access to the Internet for a fee. The ISP issues a unique userID and a secret password. You can then use the userID and password to log on to your ISP's computer that then helps you access the Internet.

The ISP computer:

◆ works with your browser to show you web pages;

◆ provides web-based e-mail and messaging services;

◆ gives access to newsgroups and chat rooms;

◆ gives users space to store their own web pages.

Mobile Internet technology

Devices with mobile Internet technology let you access the Internet while you're on the move. These devices have a built-in mobile phone to link into Internet. They have browser software and a touchscreen-driven GUI to allow easier communication. Many have other software that you would find on a palmtop such as calendar, database or a calculator.

Figure 2.6 BT Broadband status dialog box.

Figure 2.7 Blackberry mobile phone

Internet services

The Internet services you need to know about, other than the Web and e-mail, are newsgroups, chat rooms and search engines.

Newsgroups

Newsgroups are Internet discussion groups. You can join newsgroups on a wide range of subjects from art to science, religion to politics, current affairs to children's TV programs of the 1970s! To participate, users 'post' messages and other users read the messages and questions and respond if they know the answer or want to comment.

Chatrooms

Chatrooms are Internet-based discussion groups that differ from newsgroups in that they are not limited to one topic like art or science. People using chatrooms can have discussions on a wide range of topics. Also the discussion tends to be more interactive as the participants are usually all online at once.

Search engines

Search engines are used to look for web pages. A simple search has one item or topic in the search. The example below shows a search for the phrase 'computer network LAN'.

The search engine will find all the web pages related to that topic and send the results to your computer for your browser to display them. You must be careful in how you do word searches as it often only looks for the words and not the phrase. For example, the above search would display the pages with the whole phrase, but also any page with one or more of the words in them. There are a lot of pages on the Internet with the word 'computer' in them!

Figure 2.8 Google front page with search term: computer network LAN.

A **complex search** has two or more parts to the search e.g. 'Scottish mountains more than 3000 ft **not** Ben Nevis'. This search will find web pages on all Scottish mountains over 3000 ft in height apart from pages on Ben Nevis.

Using a complex search will help the search engine produce a more accurate search by producing fewer, but more precise, results.

Software available on the Internet

The Internet can be a good source of software. Sometimes the software is free, or available free for a trial period. Care should be taken in downloading software, as this is another way in which computer viruses can be spread.

Freeware

Freeware is free but the author still holds the copyright. You can use freeware and make copies to give to people. However, you must not change the software or sell it. Examples of freeware are some games, and printer drivers.

Shareware

Shareware normally has a free 30-day trial period. If you want to use the software after the 30 days you need to either register the software and pay a fee or delete the shareware.

When the fee has been paid you can then make and distribute copies. People receiving copies, in turn, have 30 days to register or delete. This is an easy way to distribute software, but some people do not pay.

Commercial software

Commercial software is software you pay for. It comes with a detailed licence agreement. You can normally make one backup copy, but you cannot lend, sell or hire the software. If you buy a single copy, you can only install it on one machine. Breaking the licence agreement breaks the Copyright, Designs and Patents Act.

Videoconferencing

Videoconferencing can be set up using a computer network to link people in distant parts of the world and allow them have face-to-face meetings without the burden of travelling. A network-based video conference transmits live audio and video signals across the network and so demands a lot of bandwidth on the network.

A simple videoconference can be set up using a webcam, microphones and speakers attached to desktops on a LAN. Many schools have set up a simple conferencing system linking people in different parts of the school.

Social issues

Access to information

The Internet is full of information on every subject from science to art and politics (but don't assume that just because it's on the Internet it's accurate!). If you have access to this information it can help you with your education, your job or even your hobbies. With access to the Internet, you can do your shopping without leaving the house, get the family holiday booked and even arrange a climbing trip with friends. Those with easy access to these services are called **information rich**. Note: this is not about the amount of money they have, it refers to the **access** to information.

Despite the fact that the Internet is freely available in most public libraries, some people have less access to the information and services offered online. These groups are said to be **information poor**. Businesses often have special offers only available on their website and some companies only advertise jobs on the web! If you don't have access to this Internet-based information you may be at a disadvantage in many ways.

Losing social contact

There is a possible problem for some people who use the Internet too much and cut themselves off from other people, communicating only through the computer system. There is a concern that they will become less able to communicate face-to-face.

Legal issues

Like any area of business, networks are used for crime. **Viruses** are planted in computer systems and **hackers** try to access customer information, including banking details, using networks. Every year billions of pounds are stolen by people using networks for credit card fraud. **Never give any security details** out over e-mail or the phone and report any attempts to gather this information. Only use reputable sites when buying on-line.

Networks are used to send **illegal copies of software**. Sites like Limewire are used to share files. A lot of these files are **illegal downloads** of music or films. Many people have been heavily fined, or imprisoned, for 'pirating' music or films in this way.

Junk mail and chain letters invade peoples' privacy. A few dozen people are responsible for over **90%** of the world's junk e-mails (known as 'spam')! They get computers to send out tens of millions of e-mails every day.

The Internet contains a lot of **unsuitable information**, some of which is illegal in the UK. Many sites record the machine address of any computer accessing data and start sending you advertising e-mails! Many people do not know that the police have the right to enter your house, take your computer and all your disks away and search them for such data.

Check out the GPP chapter for information on the **Data Protection Act**, the **Copyright, Design and Patents Act** and the **Computer Misuse Act**.

Ethical issues

Ethics is about what is right and what is wrong, not just about what is legal. There are other ways in which people use networks wrongly:

◆ being racist or sexist;
◆ breaking confidences by telling secrets;
◆ gossiping and spreading lies;
◆ starting arguments in chatrooms.

Guides to proper ethical conduct can be found in the Netiquette codes on page 44.

Most businesses have codes of conduct called ' Acceptable Use Policies'.

Questions

8. What is text messaging?

9. List 3 advantages of e-mail.

10. What is netiquette? Give three examples.

11. What is the difference between a dial-up and a broadband connection?

12. Why might a small business prefer to use a broadband connection rather than a dial-up connection?

13. What is the World Wide Web?

14. Your friend has been making up a website but finds it difficult to move between her web pages. What does she need to do to make it easy to move between the web pages?

15. What is HTML used for?

Credit

16. Give an example of a mobile Internet technology.

17. How can you transfer a file using e-mail?

18. Your friend is looking for information on large Scottish lochs near Fort William he enters 'Scottish lochs' into a search engine and gets hundreds of pages. How can he make his search more accurate?

19. A small business decides wants to market its software but it has no budget for marketing. What would be the best way to market its software?

20. Describe one **disadvantage** of **not** having access to the information on the Internet.

COMPUTER SYSTEMS

Key Words

- ★ system software
- ★ High Level Languages
- ★ portability
- ★ device drivers
- ★ directories and folders
- ★ Low Level Machine
- ★ processor
- ★ input devices

- ★ machine code
- ★ translators, interpreters and compilers
- ★ operating systems
- ★ interactive and real time processing.
- ★ sequential and random access
- ★ Input Process Output
- ★ main memory
- ★ output devices

Systems Software

Programs and computers

Computers are just big electronic boxes! They need programs to make them into useful tools. Programs are **ordered lists of instructions** written by computer programmers. The computer starts at the first instruction and carries out each instruction in turn until it is told to stop or it reaches the end of the program.

Machine code

Machine code is the language that the computer understands at the lowest level. In machine code, the instructions are made up of **binary** numbers and look like the box on the right. Programs written in machine code run *very* fast. The disadvantage is that they are very difficult for humans to read and understand.

01101101
11001100
01011100
11110000

High Level Languages

High Level Languages **(HLL)** are programming languages that are much closer to English than to the binary language of computers. They use English words and have a sentence-like structure. High Level Languages are easier to learn and use.

A typical piece of a computer program might look like this:

```
REPEAT
   INPUT "Enter age": age
UNTIL age > 0
PRINT "You are"; age;"years old"
```

Translators

Remember, at the lowest level, the system **only** understands machine code.

All programs written in a High Level Language need to be translated into machine code before the instructions can be carried out by the system. We use translator programs to carry out this translation.

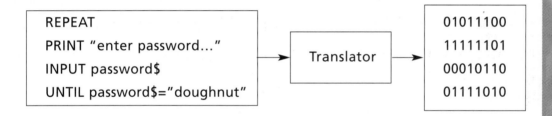

There are **two** different types of translator, each with its own advantages and disadvantages. They are **compilers** and **interpreters**.

Compiler

A **compiler** translates high level language instructions, called **source code**, into machine code, or **object code**. It does this by going through the source a line at a time and translating it. It puts the translation in a file and moves on. When the whole program is translated the object code can be run. There is no need to translate the source again, unless the program is changed. If there are any syntax errors (errors in the structure and order of the instructions), it lists them. The object cannot be run until the whole program is translated.

Advantages of a compiler:

◆   if no errors are found, then the source does not need to be translated again;

◆   the translator program is no longer required once the program is translated;

◆   object code can be distributed without having to show how software was written.

Disadvantages of a compiler:

◆   if there are **any** syntax errors present then the program will not run;

◆   the errors may be harder to correct, as problems may not be identified.

C *Interpreter*

An **interpreter** does not produce **object code**. The translator translates **and** executes **each** line of the program **in turn**.

Advantages of an interpreter:

◆ if errors are present, then they are highlighted immediately and are therefore easier to detect and fix;

◆ interpreters can run partial code or code under development.

Disadvantages of an interpreter:

◆ as the translation is **not** saved, the interpreter **must** be present to run code;

◆ if code is repeated, as in a loop, the code is translated and run **many** times;

◆ individual runs are slower, due to the above two points.

Portability of software

A program is described as **portable** if it can be run on a system other than the one on which it was written with **little or no change**.

If a program is written on one machine and then transferred to another and it runs properly it is portable. Programs written in high level languages are **more** portable than others.

Many games are written once and then fed into two or more different compilers. This means that there are EXE files, or object code, for more than one family of processors.

Questions ?

1. Why are translators necessary?

2. Why do programmers prefer using High Level Languages rather than machine code?

C Credit

3. Why does compiled software run faster than interpreted software?

4. What is portable software?

Definition of an operating system

An Operating System (**OS**) is a program, or set of programs, that controls all the tasks your computer carries out. Without the OS no other tasks could take place. It runs other software, controls peripherals and monitors the operation of the computer.

There are many different operating systems available today. Three of the most common are Microsoft Windows XP, LINUX and Apple OS X.

Figure 3.1 Icons for Windows XP and Linux.

Main functions of an operating system

An operating system has several different functions. The Standard Grade course requires that you know about **four** of them:

◆ providing the Human Computer Interface (HCI) for the user;

◆ file management;

◆ memory management;

◆ error reporting.

Providing the Human Computer Interface for the user

The operating system is responsible for displaying all the windows, icons, dialogue boxes and menus used in the interface. It also takes in user input in the form of key presses, mouse clicks and voice input. It passes these commands to other parts of the OS to be carried out. Other names given to this type of HCI are a Graphical User Interface (GUI) or a WIMP system.

File management

The **file management** system manages the loading and saving of files. It involves carrying out tasks such as:

◆ creating and deleting files;

◆ organising files into directories and sub-directories;

◆ controlling access to files (such as locking important files so they can't be changed).

Memory management

The operating system organises the use of the computer's memory. It checks there is enough room in memory for the file then loads them in. It also makes sure that files do not overlap with each other or interfere with the running of the OS.

Error reporting

The error reporting system is responsible for displaying error messages. These could be from a program being run, or from the OS itself.

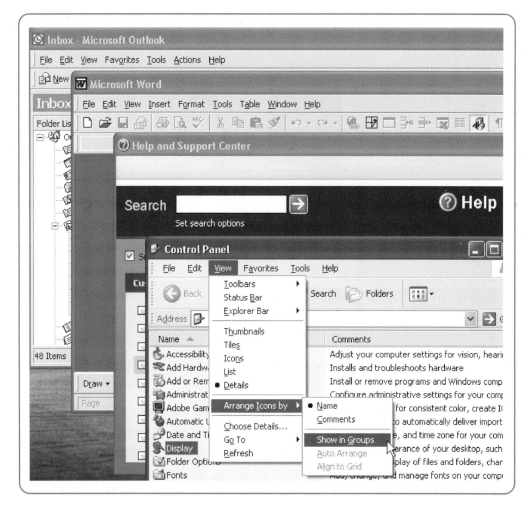

Figure 3.2 Graphical User Interface.

Interactive and real time systems

Most operating systems are described as **interactive** - the user enters a command and receives a response from the system. In a system where the computer reacts to user requests **immediately**, the system is called a **real time** system. Any system that reacts instantly to data is called a real time system (such as in aircraft control systems).

Interactive systems with background job capability

When a user wants to print a file the computer has to communicate with the printer. While it is doing this, the CPU is busy and no other work can be done. To free up the processor, many systems allow printing to be carried out as a **background task**. This means that communication with the printer will only take place if the processor is free of other tasks. The operating system juggles many tasks at once, each getting its share of the processor. Many of these are being carried out in the background, when the main task is idle.

Device drivers

Every peripheral attached to a computer works differently. They work at different speeds, using their own control codes and signals. When a manufacturer produces a new peripheral, such as a printer or a scanner, they put all the information that the operating system needs to communicate with, and control the peripheral, into a program called a **device driver**.

Some operating systems come with lots of device drivers bundled. However, there may be times when you attach a new peripheral to a system and the driver is not available in the operating system. In these cases, you need to load a driver from CD (usually provided with the peripheral device) or download it from the Internet.

Files, folders and directories

There are two types of file, a **data file** and a **program file**. Program files are the programs and applications that the system runs, like MS Word or HALO. Data files contain information used by the program files. These might be letters you have typed, or photographs and games you have saved.

When you have a lot of files to be stored it is a great help to have a system for arranging them. Storing files in one long list is not a good idea, because finding files later can be very difficult. Also, every file has to have a unique name for the user, and the system, to identify it. The best way to organise files is to group them into categories. These groups can be stored together in one **folder** or **directory**.

A **directory**, or **folder**, is a group of files that are related in some way. For example, you might have a folder for different school subjects: a Computing folder, a History folder and English folder. By changing the access rights of these folders the user can allow others to access files across a network. Your school or college may have a student file area where course files are placed by staff, and students can only read the files but not change them.

Hierarchical filing system

When you are dealing with lots of directories, it is much better to organise them into a **tree-like** structure. This is known as a **hierarchical** filing system.

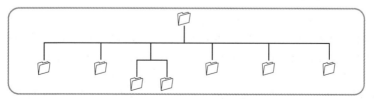

Figure 3.3 Tree structure for files.

C This system has the following advantages:

◆ more orderly structure, allowing user to find data quicker;

◆ allows user to control access to directories (so other users can only read the files and not make changes to them. Such files are called 'read-only files');

◆ allows duplicate names, so for example several files called 'report.doc' may exist in different folders.

Sequential access to data

In a system with sequential access, data is stored in sequence or order, usually by order of a key number such as an account number.

To access data the system starts at the beginning of the sequence and reads each piece of data until it locates what it needs. For example, to find a block of data on a magnetic tape the system uses sequential access. It starts at the beginning and accesses each block in turn, forwarding the tape till it reaches the data it needs.

Magnetic tape works in this way.

Direct access to data

Using **direct access**, also called **random access**, the system goes **directly** to the location in memory in which it is stored. It is much quicker to store and to access data in this way. This is the way that hard disk drives, USB flash drives, CD-RW drives, and DVD drives work.

Questions ?

5. What is a real time system used for?

6. What is the difference between a program file and a data file.

C Credit

7. List two jobs carried out by every operating system.

8. Explain how a sequential access system operates.

9. Describe file management.

10. Give two advantages of a hierarchical filing system

Low level machine

Input, Process, Output

The computer is a very complex machine that is good at doing **two** things:

◆ remembering simple instructions;

◆ carrying out calculations and instructions really fast.

All of the complex processes can be broken down into three simple stages. These are **input**, **process** and **output**. Data is taken in, something is done to or with it and then some action is taken. Some simple examples are given in the table below.

Input	Process	Output
Enter numbers into a spreadsheet	Add them up	Send to a printer
Enter names into a database	Sort them into alphabetical order	Display on a monitor
Read pressure levels from a sensor	Check if they are above required level	Set off alarm

The processor

Central to the input–process-output model is the processor, also called the microprocessor or chip. The processor is the 'brains' of the computer that deals with all the movement of data and any calculations to be carried out. A processor is a number of layers of silicon crystal wafers on which millions of tiny electronic components are etched.

The **processor** is made up of **three** important components:

◆ the Control Unit (CU);

◆ Arithmetic and Logic Unit (ALU);

◆ registers.

The **Control Unit** sends control signals to:

◆ store data in memory;

◆ fetch data from memory;

◆ decode and carry out instructions;

The Arithmetic and Logic Unit (ALU) carries out all the computers **arithmetic** and **logical** functions:

◆ arithmetic functions such as addition, subtraction, multiplication;

◆ logic functions such as comparing values using IF, AND, OR, >, <, =.

Figure 3.4 Microprocessor chip.

Registers are small **temporary** memory locations located **on the processor**. They are used to store data, instructions and memory addresses.

Computer memory

The **main memory** of a computer can be either **Random Access Memory (RAM)** or **Read Only Memory (ROM)**. **RAM** is the working space of the computer. It holds all of the programs and data files currently in use by the system and users. **ROM** is system memory. It holds vital systems information like startup instructions.

Features of **RAM**:

◆ **RAM** can exchange information with the processor at high speed;

◆ data held in **RAM** can be changed;

◆ all data in **RAM** is **lost** when the power is switched off;

◆ **RAM** holds all the data and programs currently in use.

Features of **ROM**:

◆ data is stored permanently in **ROM** and is **not lost** when the power goes off;

◆ data in the **ROM** cannot be changed;

◆ **ROM** holds vital systems data and programs.

A typical modern computer would have a minimum of 1 gigabyte of RAM and 4 megabytes of ROM. This diagram, called a memory map, shows how computer memory is divided into RAM and ROM.

RAM
User Software and Data
Operating System programs and data files
ROM
Startup data and instructions

Measuring the size of memory

We use these terms to measure the computer's memory.

bit	binary digit: a single **1** or **0**
byte	8 bits e.g. **11001110**
kilobyte	1024 bytes
megabyte	1024 kilobytes
gigabyte	1024 megabytes
terabyte	1024 gigabytes

Word

A **word** is the amount of data that the processor can move in and out of memory and manipulate at any one time, and is described as the number of bits treated as a single unit by the processor.

C If a computer has a 32 bit word it can manipulate 32 bits at a time. If a system has a 64 bit word it can manipulate 64 bits at a time.

The larger the word size, the more data that can be manipulated in one operation, the better the performance of the system. The original GameBoy had an 8 bit processor, so it could only process 8 bits at one time. The DreamCast had a 128 bit processor, so no wonder it was a lot faster!

Memory addresses

The computer's main memory is divided into many memory locations. Each location has its own unique address and each one can contain data. The processor uses the address to locate data in memory, to store data in or fetch data from memory.

Location	Contents
01111010	0111101011110010
01111001	0101010111111111
01111010	1111000010101010
01111001	0101010111100111

The maximum number of locations possible depends upon the number of bits in the address.

Storing numbers, text and graphics

Storing numbers

We use the decimal numbers 0,1,2,3,4,5,6,7,8,9.

Computers use binary numbers. To work with decimals, the computer has to convert them. The table below will help you understand how to convert them.

2^7	2^6	2^5	2^4	2^3	2^2	2^1	2^0	power of 2
128	64	32	16	8	4	2	1	decimal equivalent

The decimal number 66 is stored as **01000010** in binary.

2^7	2^6	2^5	2^4	2^3	2^2	2^1	2^0	power of 2
128	64	32	16	8	4	2	1	decimal
0	1	0	0	0	0	1	0	= 64 +2 = 66

Text

Text is represented using **ASCII** code. **ASCII** stands for **A**merican **S**tandard **C**ode for **I**nformation **I**nterchange. Each of the characters in the character set, all the characters available to the user, has a unique value.

All characters are included:

◆ upper and lower case letters e.g. A-Z, a-z;

◆ numbers 0 – 9;

◆ punctuation and other symbols ($ & * ^ @ " :) ;

◆ non-printing characters like <return>, <tab>, <escape>.

An extract of the binary code is shown here:

Binary	Decimal	Representing
01000001	65	A
01000010	66	B
01000011	67	C
01000100	68	D
01000101	69	E
01000110	70	F

Graphics

Graphics (drawings, graphs or pictures) are made up of **pixels**, or points on the screen.

Each pixel is represented by patterns of binary numbers where each square or pixel filled in = 1, each square or pixel left blank = 0.

C ### Calculating the storage space for black and white graphics

Graphics files can be very big and need a lot of memory to store them. To know the size of memory needed for one image, you need to calculate the number of pixels in the image. In the example above, the image measures 8 pixels wide and 8 pixels high, so:

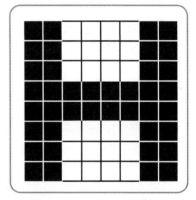

Figure 3.5 Simple 8 × 8 bitmap image.

◆ the number of pixels is 8 × 8 = 64 pixels

◆ each pixel in black and white requires 1 bit to store it = 64 bits

◆ memory is expressed in bytes, so divide by 8 for bytes, 64/8 = 8 bytes

Graphics tend to be much larger than this simple example, particularly when the images are in colour.

Calculate the size of a graphic which is 6 inches by 6 inches at 300 pixels per inch.

◆ 1800 × 1800 pixels = 3 240 000 pixels

◆ for a black and white graphic = 3 240 000 bits

- to convert from bits to bytes, divide by 8: 3 240 000/8 = 405 000 bytes
- to convert from bytes to kilobytes, divide by 1024: 405 000/1024 = **395.5 kilobytes**

Questions

11. What is a processor?
12. List two differences between RAM and ROM.
13. What is the ASCII code used for?

Credit

14. Calculate the storage requirements for a black and white graphic 8 inches × 6 inches at 300 pixels per inch. Answer in kilobytes.

Types of computer system

Desktop computer

A **desktop computer** is made up of a system unit which holds the processor, main memory, hard disk drive, CD and DVD drives, and a separate monitor, keyboard and mouse. A desktop is reasonably compact and will fit onto a workstation or desk.

Figure 3.6 Desktop computer showing monitor, computer, keyboard and mouse.

Laptop computer (notebook)

Laptop, or **notebook**, computers have all the same components as a desktop (except the mouse), but they are all packaged into one small portable unit. Laptops have these features:

- small enough to use on your lap comfortably;
- useful for working away from the home or office;
- takes up little space and can be carried easily;

Figure 3.7 Laptop computer.

COMPUTER SYSTEMS

63

◆ light, weighing less than 4 kg;

◆ powered by batteries (or by mains adapter);

◆ has a flat LCD or TFT screen;

◆ has a standard keyboard as well as a range of disk drives.

Palmtop computer

A **palmtop** computer is a small computer designed to fit in your hand or pocket. It is also called a **handheld** or a **personal data assistant (PDA)**. They are used for storing and retrieving data, keeping a diary of appointments, as an MP3 player, communicating with a network and a host of other uses. Palmtops are merging with mobile phones to produce 'smartphones' (see page 47).

A palmtop has these features:

◆ smaller than a laptop (it fits onto your hand);

◆ very light (weighing less than 200g);

Figure 3.8 Palmtop computer.

◆ small, on screen, keyboard;

◆ has a touch sensitive screen;

◆ has a full range of GPPs, (although they are usually cut-down versions of the software on desktop or laptop computers);

◆ may allow the user to input using a pen (or stylus);

◆ powered by a small battery;

◆ stores data on a flashcard.

Mainframe computer

A **mainframe computer** is a very large computer which has powerful processors, large internal memory capacity and access to backing storage media which can store large volumes of data. Mainframes work at high speeds, accessing and storing data as well as processing transactions.

They often have many terminals connected to the processor and allow many people to use the system at the same time – this is called multi-access. Multi-access computers are so powerful and fast that that users may not be aware that they are sharing the

Figure 3.9 Mainframe computer.

system with lots of others. Banks, mail order companies, universities and other large organisations use mainframes.

Multimedia computers

Multimedia systems incorporate and integrate sound, animated images, video and graphics within a single user-friendly computer interface. The user can interact with and access text, video clips, sound tracks, still and animated graphics. They are used to provide interactive learning systems and information systems as well as games.

Input devices for a multimedia system may include:

- microphone
- digital camera
- digital video camera
- scanner
- CD player
- radio tuner

Using a MIDI interface, a musical instrument can be played directly into a computer. Sound, video and graphics data can also be downloaded from the Internet and incorporated into a multimedia presentation.

Output devices for a multimedia system include:

- high resolution monitor
- surround sound speakers
- data projector
- musical instrument (using a MIDI interface a computer can output directly to an electronic instrument such as an electronic keyboard or a synthesiser).

Sound and graphics cards

Sound and graphics cards are specialised pieces of hardware to process sound or graphics images. They contain a processor and memory and are plugged directly into your processor motherboard. Sound and graphics cards help the performance of computers by freeing up the main computer processor so that it can get on with other tasks. A good graphics card can speed up game play on a PC, as the main processor no longer needs to work out what the screen should look like and display it. A mid-range graphics card will have 256 megabytes of RAM.

What you need to know about input devices

A number of input devices are commonly available to the user:

- keyboard
- graphics tablet
- touch sensitive screen
- mouse
- trackball
- trackpad
- scanner
- digital camera
- microphone

Keyboard

The keyboard is used to type text and enter commands into the system. The keyboard contains a set of the usual *qwerty* keys as well as special command and function keys.

Mouse

A mouse is a pointing device which lets the user interact with the computer system. The hand-sized case of the mouse has at least one button on top and a ball fitted underneath. Sensors detect the movement of the ball and the button. The mouse is used to control the cursor on the screen and to manipulate icons and menus.

Trackball

A trackball serves the same purpose as a mouse, but it works slightly differently. The ball and buttons are both on the top of the case and the case is not moved. Instead, the ball is rolled by the hand. It is suitable for uses where fine control of the cursor is required such as detailed design work.

Figure 3.10 Mouse.

Trackpad

A trackpad is another device which serves the same purpose as a mouse, but this time they are used on laptop computers. The trackpad is a small pad with sensors that detect the movements and taps of your finger. This lets the user control the position of the pointer on the screen and select icons and open menus. Trackpads are more convenient when using a laptop on the move where it is difficult to use a mouse.

Figure 3.11 Trackball.

Joystick

Joysticks are used mainly in games to give the user control over the game objects like a car, a plane or a human character. Controlling a game using a joystick is much easier than using the keyboard and mouse.

Graphics tablet

A graphics tablet is a flat pad with electronic sensors below the surface. These detect the movements of a pointing device (stylus) and move the cursor on the screen accordingly. This system has the advantage of being very sensitive and accurate and is used in engineering and design systems.

Figure 3.12 Graphics tablet.

Touch sensitive screen

A touch sensitive monitor screen can detect fingers or pointers touching its surface. Simply by touching the screen the user can make a selection or move the position of the cursor. They are simple to operate making them suitable for a wide range of applications, and you may have seen them on tills in shops and restaurants as well as public information systems. However they are not suitable for tasks that demand precision input.

Scanner

A scanner enables the user to capture image, like photos or documents, onto the computer in a digital form. The scanner works by shining a light on the document and reading where the light reflect, the white bits. This information is changes into binary values for light and dark and saves the file.

Figure 3.13 Scanner.

Digital camera

A digital camera is a device for taking digital pictures. It is like a conventional camera except that instead of recording the image using film, the image is captured digitally and stored on a memory card. One measure of the quality of a digital camera is the number of megapixels used to record the image – this is the number of millions of detectors in the grid that detects the picture. A good one will have an 8 megapixels sensor and will cost more than £200. Advantages of digital cameras include the large number of images you can store without film, and you can delete the pictures you don't want, and the pictures you do want can be transferred to a computer and printed them out.

Figure 3.14 Digital camera.

Microphone

Microphones capture sound data and transmit it to the computer for storing. Most computers have built-in microphones, but these are not usually of a high quality.

Webcam

Webcams are digital cameras which are used to take photos to be transferred to a web page and then sent across the Internet. They can be used for viewing traffic flowing along motorways, for advertising tourist attractions and for advertising business sites.

Specialised forms of input for virtual reality

Virtual reality systems use a range of *specialised input devices*. These may be built into special gloves, helmets and even suits which the user wears. The devices can include ultrasound transmitters in gloves and suits to track the user's movements, and strips built into gloves that vary their resistance when bent. These sensors send data about the user's movements to the processor.

Specialised forms of input for disabled people

Disabled people may not be able to use the common input devices, so specialised devices have been developed. **Biosensors** are used to detect movements in muscles and eyes. These enable people to control a computer by simply twitching a muscle or moving their eye.

Figure 3.15 Virtual Reality helmet.

Special mouse devices controlled by head movements are available. These work by passing signals between a device on the user's forehead to manipulate the cursor and control the computer system.

A **touchpad** detects the pressure of your hand on the pad and so allows a user to select icons and open windows. Unlike a trackpad, it does not detect movement.

It is often used as an input device by people with a disability who cannot click a mouse.

There are **specialised keyboards** and **screens** available for people with speech difficulties. These are often called **concept keyboards**.

Sound cards

Computer systems use **sound cards** to capture **audio** data. Sound cards do this by taking tens of thousands of samples of the analogue sound waves each second. They then change each sample into a binary number and store each sample in memory.

This can make very heavy demands on the processor and memory. For example if a sound is sampled at 44kHz the processor has to convert 44 000 analogue quantities to binary form every second and then store each one.

Sound cards have their own on-board processors and memory units to take the strain off the computers own processor and main memory. Without a sound card the system would slow down

Questions

15. Write down two key features of a mainframe?

16. Give two uses for a palmtop.

17. Why do you finds trackpads on laptops?

18. Why would an artist use a graphics tablet rather than a mouse to draw on a computer system?

19. Give two advantages of a digital camera.

20. Give two uses of a webcam.

Credit

21. Write down two forms of input that are designed for use by disabled people.

22. How does a sound card work?

What you need to know about output devices

A number of output devices are commonly available:

- printers
- monitors
- plotters
- loudspeakers

Laser printer

Laser printers work by using a laser beam to put the image of a page onto a photosensitive drum. The toner or ink then sticks to the charged drum. This is then transferred to paper and fused by heat to make it stick.

Figure 3.16 Laser printer.

They are very fast and produce very high quality output. However, they can be more expensive to buy than an inkjet.

Inkjet printer

Inkjet printers sprays ink onto paper to form letters and pictures. It produces high quality output and is less expensive to buy than a laser printer. However, running costs can be high as the ink cartridges can be expensive (and it dries out if you don't use it often). They are also a lot slower than laser printers.

Figure 3.17 Inkjet printer.

Comparing printers

You can compare printers according to the following criteria…

Speed	This is measured in pages per minute (ppm) e.g. 8 ppm.
Resolution	The higher the resolution, the more dots per inch (dpi), the better the quality of the printout. Printouts from a printer capable of 900 dpi will be poorer in quality than those from a 1200 dpi printer.
Cost	Capital cost: the initial cost of buying the printer. Running costs: cost of toner or ink (and paper).

Plotter

A plotter is used to draw line-based graphics such as diagrams, charts, plans. Many plotters use the same technology as inkjet printers.

Monitor

The screen used to display computer output is called a **monitor**, also **display** or **VDU**. Different monitors have different resolutions, different quality. The higher the resolution the clearer the image. High resolution monitors are needed for CAD work and art work.

There are 3 types of monitor: **Cathode Ray Tubes** (CRT) which use old technology and are quite bulky, and **Liquid Crystal Display** and **Thin Film Transistor** screens. The last two are flat screens, and take up less space and energy than CRT screens.

Liquid Crystal Display (LCD)

LCD screens use transistors and a thin film of liquid crystals and to control the light passing through the screen. They are often found on palmtop and laptop computers because they are light, compact and need little power and can be run on batteries. One problem is that some LCD screens are not very bright and can cause eyestrain if they are used for too long.

Thin Film Transistor (TFT)

TFT is a type of LCD screen that uses lots of transistors to produce a high quality display. A TFT screen can display animations and 3 dimensional graphics much more clearly than ordinary LCD screens. The disadvantage is that they are a lot more expensive than ordinary LCD screens.

Loudspeakers

Loudspeakers enable your computer to output music, multimedia presentations with voice-overs and sound effects, videos and even discussions on a video conference link. Most PCs come with a small set of speakers fitted, but for better quality you can buy a full set of loudspeakers.

Specialised forms of output for disabled people

Text output as speech

People with disabilities that make it difficult to read or to speak can use software to output the text files as speech.

Using ultrasound and infrared

Using ultrasound and infrared output devices attached to computers it is possible to control machinery and even domestic appliances such as TV, DVD players, microwaves, telephones and lights. These forms of output are very useful to people with disabilities.

Specialised output for virtual reality

The output from a virtual reality system creates a 3-dimensional world for the user. The user feels *immersed* inside the virtual world created by the computer. This is achieved by using a pair of small but high definition screens which are usually set into a headset, such as a helmet or visor, which the user wears.

The 3-D effect of the screens in the headset is added to by the surround sound produced by speakers. The overall effect is to make the user feel part of the computer's world, part of the virtual reality.

Backing storage devices

This category covers all storage devices outside of the main CPU. Here are the main types of storage devices:

- Magnetic tapes
- Floppy Disks
- Hard disks
- CD-ROM
- CD-R
- CD-RW
- DVD-ROM
- DVD-R
- DVD-Rewritable
- Zip Disks
- USB Flash Drive

Tape

Plastic magnetic tapes, like audio or video tapes, store data in binary using magnetic 'spots' to encode the data. Tapes are often used for making backups and use sequential access to data (see page 58).

Advantages of tape storage include:

- cheaper than other forms of storage;
- large capacity, they can hold hundreds of Gigabytes of data;
- fast data transfer rates.

Disadvantages of tape storage include:

- slower to access than a hard disk because access is sequential;
- tape can degrade, leading to loss of data over time (so best used for medium and short term storage);
- damaged easily by heat, dust, dampness, electromagnetic fields.

Floppy disk

Floppy disks are cheap magnetic storage devices with a limited storage capacity. High density disks hold 1.44 Megabytes of data.

Advantages of floppy disks include:

◆ small in size and easy to handle;

◆ cheap per disk;

◆ portable.

Disadvantages of floppy disks include:

◆ damaged easily by heat, dust, dampness, electromagnetic fields;

◆ small capacity.

Hard disk

The hard disk is the main memory in most computers. It is a metal disk with magnetised surfaces on which data is stored as patterns of magnetic spots. They are in sealed units to stop dust and dirt corrupting data. They are usually fixed in the computer, but you can get portable external drives.

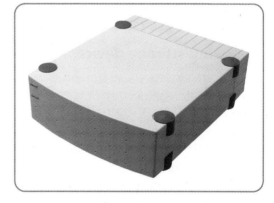

Advantages of hard disks include:

◆ fast access times, direct access;

◆ fast data transfer rates;

◆ cheap per megabyte.

Disadvantages of hard disks include:

◆ not usually portable;

◆ can be damaged if dropped.

Figure 3.18 Hard disk drive.

CD-ROM

CD-ROM stands for **Compact Disk – Read Only Memory**. It is an example of optical storage. It is fast and can store up to 650 Mb of data. The data on the CD-ROM is fixed at time of manufacture and it cannot be written to. The data is read by a sensor that detects laser light reflected from the surface of the disk.

The speed of a CD drive is measured by the transfer rate of a packet of 150 kilobits, so for example, a CD drive marked **52x** will transfer 52 × 150 kilobits per second.

CD-R

CD-R stands for **CD-recordable**. CD-R disks can be recorded on once. Once data is recorded on it, it works just like a CD-ROM, and is a read-only disk. They can store up to 650 Mb. The speed of a CD-R drive is given as two numbers, the **read** speed and the **write** speed.

CD-RW

CD-RW stands for **CD-rewriteable**. CD-RW disks are disks on which you can record data over and over again, just like hard disks. You can use them to make backups of large files, such as groups of photos, and you can change the data stored on the disk as often as you want. A CD-RW has three speeds, for **writing** data, for **re-writing** and for **reading**. For example, a disk might be specified as: **write 52X**, **re-write 24X** and **read 52X**.

DVD-ROM

A **DVD-ROM** uses optical technology to read data. Like a CD-ROM it is a read-only disk. A DVD-ROM has much larger data **capacity** than a CD-ROM. Single-sided single-layered DVDs have a capacity of 4.7 Gigabytes. Double-sided multi-layered DVDs have a capacity of 17 Gigabytes. The speed of a DVD-ROM drive is measured in the same way as a CD drive, but in the case of DVDs, the speed is measured by the transfer rate of a packet of 1250 kilobits, so a DVD drive marked **16X** will transfer at a rate of 16 x 1250 kilobits per second.

DVD-R

DVD-R stands for **DVD Recordable**. Just like CD-R, this allows you to record data once on a DVD. After recording the data cannot be changed. DVD-R disks have the same capacity as DVDs but have two speeds, for **writing** and for **reading** data, such as **write 6X**, **read 12X**

DVD-RW

DVD-RW stands for **DVD Rewriteable**. This is a DVD that allows you to record data over and over again. Like hard disks, you can use them to make backups of **very** large files, such as home movies from your digital video camera, and you can change the data stored on the disk as often as you want. A DVD-RW has three speeds, for **writing** data, for **re-writing** and for **reading** such as **write 6X**, **re-write 2.4X** and **read 12X**.

USB Flash drive

Also called a pen drive or memory stick, a flash drive is a small portable backing storage device with no moving parts. Flash drives can store large amounts of data, up to 4 Gb. They simply plug into the USB ports on your computer and are a convenient way of making backups and of transferring data between computers.

Figure 3.19 USB pen drive.

Comparing backing storage devices

You need to be able to compare backing storage devices according to their **capacity**, **speed of data transfer** and **cost**. Copy and complete a table like the one below using the latest information from magazines and the Internet.

Type of backing storage	Name and model	Capacity	Speed of data transfer	Cost per Megabyte
Tape drive				
Floppy disk				
Hard disk				
USB flash drive				
CD-ROM				
CD-R				
CD-RW				
DVD-ROM				
DVD-RW				

Types of data access

The **two** types of data access you have to know about are **sequential access** and **random access**, also called **direct access**.

Sequential access is used for magnetic tape. It means that when you want a specific piece of data that is halfway through the tape, you have to wind all the way through before you can read it.

In **random**, or **direct access** the read head goes straight to the address where the data is held, so there is no waiting time while the disk scans through earlier data.

To give an example, if you were trying to play track 5 of your favourite album on CD you would jump straight to the track and play it. If the album is on tape, you would have to wait while the tape drive fast-forwarded to the start of track 5.

Questions

23. Give one advantage and one disadvantage of a laser printer.

24. List two disadvantages of an inkjet printer.

25. How is the resolution of a printer measured?

26. How does a TFT screen differ from an ordinary LCD screen?

27. Describe the difference in capacity between a DVD-ROM and a CD-ROM?

28. What are DVDs mainly used for?

29. Describe a USB flash drive.

Credit

30. Why are graphic cards necessary?

31. Describe two forms of output for a virtual reality system.

32. What type of backing storage uses sequential access?

33. What is sequential access?

COMMERCIAL DATA PROCESSING

Key Words

- ★ **processing systems**
- ★ **data processing cycle**
- ★ **EFTPoS**
- ★ **data security**

- ★ **management information**
- ★ **E-commerce**
- ★ **computer crime and fraud**

Commercial data processing systems

Commercial data processing is the use of powerful computer systems to collect and process large volumes of data at high speed.

There are many good reasons for using commercial data processing systems, including:

- large amounts of data can be processed. A bank's computer system can process hundreds of thousands of pieces of data every hour;

- **repetitive tasks** are handled easily. Computers in a bank can produce customer account statements repeating the same process over and over again without making an error;

- data is processed at **high speeds**. Account details are updated instantly;

- data is kept **accurately**. All data on customer accounts is extremely accurate;

- data is **instantly accessible**. Bank staff can call up customers account details instantly.

Managing information

A CDP system can help those **managing** the business to get instant access to the information which is central to the smooth running of the business or organisation.

In large organisations with lots of staff divided into different departments, managers need to direct and co-ordinate the work being carried out. In order to do this effectively they must be able to manage the information that is made available to all levels of staff.

C Single-entry multiple use of data

Once data is entered into a CDP system it is available to many people in the organisation. In a bank, once data about an account withdrawal is entered it is available to any teller in any branch of the bank and indeed to the bank manager as well as the customer.

Hardware

Many large organisations use a **mainframe**, a powerful central computer connected to a series of **terminals**. See page 64 for more details on mainframes.

Data and information

In its raw unprocessed form **data** has little meaning or use. Once it has been processed it becomes more meaningful and has a great deal more use and value and can be called **information**. The number **060220031504** is a piece of data, but it doesn't mean very much on its own. It is only when you know how to read it that it becomes information. Knowing that it is a date and time means that you can read it as four minutes past three in the afternoon on the sixth of February 2003!

data + context = information

The Data Processing Cycle

Commercial data processing follows the stages of the **data processing cycle**:

1. collecting, preparing and entering the data;
2. checking the data;
3. processing and storing the data;
4. information output.

Collecting, preparing and entering the data

Commercial data processing involves the collection and entry of large volumes of data. It is important to be able to enter this data swiftly and without errors. The following methods are used to speed up the entry of data.

Magnetic stripes

Magnetic stripes are found on credit cards, debit cards and even ferry tickets! Important data is stored on a piece of magnetic tape stuck to the back of the card. The card is swiped through a reader that reads the magnetic pattern on the stripe and inputs the data directly to the computer.

Figure 4.1 Ferry ticket showing magnetic strip.

The data on the card tells the computer the account details of the holder. Using a magnetic stripe is a simple, quick and accurate way to enter this data.

You need to take care of your card, as criminals can copy the details from the stripe and make a copy of your card. This is called *cloning* and is a source of credit card fraud.

Bar codes

A **bar code** consists of a pattern of wide and narrow vertical bars representing binary numbers. The code is read into the computer by passing a laser over the code and sensing the light reflected back.

ISBN 0-340-92650-3

9 780340 926505

Figure 4.2 Bar code

Mark sense cards

The mark sense system is used for collecting and entering simple responses. The card has a series of blank boxes and the user marks or colours them to indicate the choice. The most obvious example of its use is in the National Lottery.

Figure 4.3 National Lottery entry form.

Magnetic Ink Character Recognition (MICR)

The MICR system is used by banks to read account details on the bottom of cheques. The characters show the cheque number, account number and bank branch code. The characters are made from magnetised ink and are read using a scanner.

Figure 4.4 Magnetic Ink Character Recognition

Smartcards

In place of a magnetic stripe, **smartcards** have a microchip and on-board memory. More data can be held on this chip and they are harder to fake. This means smartcards are more secure and less open to computer crime.

Figure 4.5 Credit cards showing the microchip and magnetic strip.

Optical Character Recognition (OCR)

Optical Character Recognition (OCR) is the production of a text file using automatic recognition of written or printed text. It works by the following stages:

◆ scanning the text

◆ comparing the shape of each character to a list of templates

◆ output the character to a text file

Checking the data

Once the data item has been entered it must be checked to see if it is correct. There are a number of methods for checking data.

Presence checks

Presence checks ensure that a data item has been entered in a given field so that essential fields like account numbers, and e-mail address fields cannot be left blank. If nothing is entered an error message is displayed.

Check field length

Field length checks are used to count the number of characters in each field and make sure this is correct. For example, a PIN must have four digits, so a field length check would report an error if anything longer or shorter than four digits was entered.

Check field type

Field type checks ensure that the entry is of the correct datatype. Examples of this kind include checking that only characters are entered into a name field or that that only numbers are entered as a PIN.

Range check

Range checks ensure that the number entered is within a given range. Examples of a range check include checking that the entry in a month field is a whole number between 1 and 12 inclusive or the entry in a gender field is either **M** or **F**.

Check digit

A check digit is a digit whose value can be calculated from the other digits in the number. This check digit can then be used to check the accuracy of the number it is attached to.

An example is a 6 digit account number where the last number should equal the total of the previous 5 divided by the first number and rounded down to the nearest integer. So the account number 34672 would have a check digit calculated as follows:

- 34672 totals to 22;
- 22 divided by 3 equals 7.3333;
- rounding down gives 7

The system will thus expect the full number to be 346727. If any other combination is entered it will be rejected.

Verification

Verification checks whether the data entered is **accurate**. If data passes a verification check then it is accepted as true. A simple form of data verification takes place when a system asks an operator to confirm details of the data displayed on the screen by a simple *'Is this correct Y/N?'* message.

HOW TO PASS STANDARD GRADE COMPUTING STUDIES

A more complex method involves two operators typing the same data independently. The computer then reads both sets of data and compares them. If it detects any inconsistencies between them it signals an error and asks for the data to be re-entered.

Validation

A **validation** check is performed on entered data, if the data fails the check it must be re-entered. If data passes the check then it is valid, but it only *might* be true. An example of this is the range check on gender, data would pass if either M or F was entered but that does not mean that the correct letter was entered.

Both verification and validation aim to cut down on errors in data entry. Validation is easier to do automatically as part of the entry system. Verification slows the whole process down.

> **Verification Screen**
>
> > Enter amount
>
> > 20
>
> > 20 withdrawn
>
> > Y
>
> > Are you really sure?

Figure 4.6 A validation check on a bank ATM.

Questions

1. a) Which type of business is most likely to use MICR?

   b) How will a MICR system help prevent fraud?

2. What are mark sense cards used for?

3. How do bar codes speed up data entry at a POS terminal?

Credit

4. When data is entered it is essential that it is verified and validated.

   a) How would you organise the verification process?

   b) List three validation checks that could be built into the system.

Processing and storing the data

Once the data is entered into the computer the next stage is that of processing the data. The first step is to organise the data into **files**, **records** and **fields**. Each file is made up of a number of records. Each record holds the data on one item in the database and contains several fields. See the database section in Chapter 1 for detail on this.

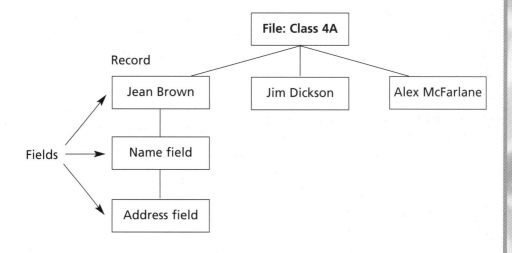

Updating information

In a large business or organisation the data held in files is constantly being updated. For example, data held on file in a bank's computer system is constantly changing as customers withdraw and deposit money.

Backups

Making backup copies is essential in case data is lost or corrupted. Backups should be made regularly and the backup held separately from the original. A typical backup strategy for a small business would be to make a copy on tape or CD-R of all the important files at the end of each working day and keep these for a week. It would also be sensible to make a copy at the end of each week and keep these backups for longer. If data is lost due to machine failure or user error then it can be recovered from these backups.

Interactive system

With interactive processing the computer reacts to user requests and processes the necessary data. For example, when a travel agent books your holiday, the booking details are processed when they are entered and the system updates its files and prints out the details of the booking.

Multi-user database

A multi-user database is one that allows many users to access the data files at the same time. Large organisations have their databases accessible to many employees over their networks. Many companies take orders via multi-user databases available over the Internet.

Sequential file access

Sequential access means that each record in the file is read one after another in sequence. **Magnetic tape** is a sequential access medium, commonly used for making backups.

Random access

This type of access enables a system to go directly to the data required. This means that it is a faster access method. Any CDP system that requires immediate update of files will use **random access**.

Output of data

Once data has been entered, processed and stored it can be output in several ways. For example order forms, receipts, customer account statements can be printed out or displayed on a monitor.

Data can also be output to file where it is stored and archived.

Social implications

Commercial data processing systems employ many different types of people. Some of the jobs and careers are described here.

Systems analyst

This person is involved in designing new systems or improving existing ones. Systems analysis involves the following tasks:

◆ deciding which tasks the system has to carry out;

◆ defining types of data needed and the processes to be carried out on that data;

◆ noting the information needed by the business or organisation.

The analyst may also be involved in the design of new software or the recommending of hardware such as including processors, input, output and backing storage devices.

Programmer

Programmers follow the instructions of the analyst to write new software and make changes to existing software.

Systems engineer

Systems engineers install and maintain the system. This includes laying the network cables, installing new printers and upgrading machines.

Network manager

The network manager runs the all or part of the network. The main tasks include:

◆ controlling access to the system;

◆ setting up user accounts, including issuing IDs and passwords;

◆ controlling access to files by setting permissions;

◆ checking that any new software and hardware are compatible with the existing system before installing them on the network.

E-commerce

People increasingly use networks, like the Internet, to buy and sell goods and services. This is type of trading of goods and services on-line is known as **e-commerce.** Apart from allowing sellers to advertise and customers to browse, e-commerce allows bidding, ordering and even paying for purchases on-line.

On-line shopping

There are websites you can browse and order any type of goods from cars to DIY, from books to houses. You can book your own holiday or order your groceries. There are even sites where you can sell your own goods and join in auctions bidding for goods.

On-line banking

You can use the Internet to contact your bank or building society and carry out a whole range of financial business such as:

- Checking your balance
- Apply for a new account
- Order a cheque book
- Set up a standing order

- Pay your bills
- Arrange a loan or mortgage
- View your statement
- Transfer money between accounts

Advantages of e-commerce

For the **customer** the advantages of e-commerce include:

- browsing for goods anytime you want, 24/7;
- ordering and paying for goods without having to leave the house;
- taking advantage of special online deals;
- shopping around for the best price without leaving your desk!

For **businesses** the advantages of e-commerce include:

- keeping costs to a minimum as there is no need to pay for shops or wages;
- selling to a **mass market** by using the Internet;
- instant cash flow from online payment without the need to process cheques or cash.

Electronic Funds Transfer

Electronic Funds Transfer (**EFT**) is the use of computer systems to transfer money between bank accounts. This means that no cash changes hands. The customer does not have to carry cash, the shop staff spend less time cashing up at the end of the day and there is less actual cash being carried to the bank. Another advantage to the shop is that the money from the customer is put into the shop's bank account immediately.

Point of Sale (**POS**) terminals are used in shops. Data about sales is entered at a terminal often using a barcode reader. The data is sent from to a computer which records the sales and updates stock levels. The use of smartcards to pay for groceries at a **POS** terminal in a supermarket is an example of **EFT**.

Computer Crime and Fraud

Businesses using CDP systems have to be aware of the possibility of computer crime such as copying or deleting important data or stealing money from bank accounts. The most common type of fraud is the identity theft where people steal IDs and passwords, make fake cards and then take money out of accounts.

Sale of customer lists

Businesses using CDP systems often sell **lists of their customers** to other businesses. This means that customers could receive loads of junk mail or junk e-mail. You need to read the small print on all the application forms you fill in and tick the box that says 'I do not want my details passed on to other companies'.

Accuracy of data

It is important for businesses to make sure that all the data that is kept on their system is accurate, especially customers' details. This is covered in the Data Protection Act (see page 37).

Security

In order to make sure that people do not hack into their data businesses and organisations must make sure that their CDP systems are surrounded by proper physical and system security.

Physical security measures include:

- identity cards or keys to allow access to computer rooms;
- locks on terminals;
- terminals with no removable storage drives;
- backup copies of data.

System security measures include:

- use of usernames and passwords;
- multi-level access, where some data can only be accessed by senior staff;
- encryption of sensitive data;
- audit software to keep track of all changes.

Costs

Costs can be divided into **initial costs** and **running costs.**

Initial costs are costs incurred when the system is **first set up**. These include:

- wages of systems analysts, programmers and engineers;

- training costs for staff on the new system;
- cost of the actual hardware and software;
- purchase of suitable furniture;
- alterations to buildings (for new ventilation, lighting and power sockets).

Running costs are the costs of keeping the system going. These include:

- staff wages;
- power and telecommunications costs;
- consumables such as printer paper and toner;
- cost of maintaining the hardware and software.

Why meet these costs?

Businesses are quite happy to pay this money out because CDP systems are very efficient and make businesses more profitable in the long run. There is better information on how the business is performing and overall running costs are reduced. E-commerce has revolutionised the way we shop and the way some companies do business. Information held by companies is more likely to be accurate and if not, it is easier to correct. Huge customer lists can be maintained, and these can have information on preferences that allows companies to target future sales more accurately.

Once data is entered into a CDP system by an operator, it is stored centrally. Many people can then access the information. This is called **single entry multiple use.** A good example of this is in holiday bookings. A file describing a holiday with lots of information and graphics is set up by one person. The same file can then be viewed by thousands of people trying to book holidays. Previously there were a lot of double bookings due to multiple copies of the file and holidays being sold more than once.

Questions

5. Why are backups essential?

6. Why does a travel agent's computer use an interactive system?

7. List three jobs of a network manager.

8. List three jobs of a systems analyst.

9. What is e-commerce?

10. What is EFT?

Questions continued ➤

Questions *continued*

11. List three things you can do with on-line banking.

12. Give two advantages of e-commerce for a customer and two advantages for a business.

13. Write down two initial and two running costs.

Credit

14. What is a multi-user database?

15. Why is single entry multiple use such a big advantage of commercial data processing systems?

AUTOMATED SYSTEMS

Key Words

* ★ **mobile and stationary robots**
* ★ **Computer Aided Design**
* ★ **sensors**
* ★ **simulation**
* ★ **embedded systems**
* ★ **guidance systems**
* ★ **Computer Aided Manufacture**
* ★ **Analogue to Digital conversion**
* ★ **Virtual reality**
* ★ **intelligent robots**

What is an automated system?

Automated systems are engineering and industrial systems which use computers to control machinery or other equipment. Automated systems are used for many things such as:

* ◆ controlling machinery in factories;
* ◆ controlling traffic lights;
* ◆ guiding aircraft, and trains.

Automated systems take many forms, the most common of which are robots. Robots, despite what Hollywood would have us believe, rarely look like human beings. Robots are machines designed to carry out tasks that we choose not to do ourselves. The word 'robot' comes from the Czechoslovakian word 'robata', which means slave.

Figure 5.1 A cartoon robot.

Reasons for using automated systems

Automated systems have a number of benefits and advantages compared with human operators:

* ◆ **They operate at high speeds**. A system designed to monitor pressures in storage tanks in an oil refinery will react **instantly** should pressures rise to dangerous levels, carrying out safety measures and setting off alarms.

◆ **They can handle repetitive tasks without making mistakes**. In a factory making circuits boards a human operator would eventually lose concentration and begin to make mistakes.

◆ **They are accurate and carry out tasks precisely**. Automated systems follow precisely the instructions in the programs that control them. This guarantees 100% accuracy in whatever task they carry out.

◆ **They work in dangerous places** such as near nuclear reactors, on North Sea oil platforms, in chemical factories.

◆ **They are efficient**. They are very efficient, because they do not make mistakes and because they waste no time or materials.

◆ **They can work continuously for long periods of time**. They can work 24/7, without taking tea-breaks or holidays!

◆ **They are adaptable.** They can be equipped with a range of sensors to help them detect their surroundings. Different tools can be fitted to them and they can be re-programmed to carry out a wide range of tasks. Some of the tools used are magnets, welding torches, spray guns, grippers, suction cups.

Stationary robots

Some robots are **stationary**, so they are fixed in one spot to perform a task so a robot arm in a factory might weld parts onto a car body.

In this course, you are expected to know about the four **mobile joints** found in most robot arms. These are *wrist, elbow, waist* and *shoulder*. The part at the end is called the *tool*.

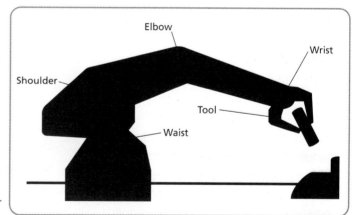

Figure 5.2 Articulated robot arm.

Mobile robots

Other robots are **mobile**. They have motors and wheels or tracks. A mobile robot might be used for transporting goods around a warehouse or factory.

How do mobile robots find their way about?
We will look at two methods for guiding robots: **magnetic fields** and **light guides**.

Magnetic guidance system

In a **magnetic guidance system**, electricity is run through a cable set in the factory floor which gives off a magnetic field. The robot is fitted with sensors that detect the field and feed the data back to the processor. The processor controls the wheels to make sure the robot follows the buried cable. The detection system is similar to the device that is used to detect pipes and wires in a wall before hammering in a nail!

Light guidance system

A **light guidance system** works in a similar way to magnetic guidance system, but in this case, the sensors detect reflected light instead of a magnetic field. The robot follows a white line painted on the factory floor. The robot shines a light onto the line. Sensors on either side of the light source measure the amount of light bouncing back. If the robot goes off to the left of the line, the readings from the left sensor fall and the processor sends control signals to the wheels to correct the course of the robot.

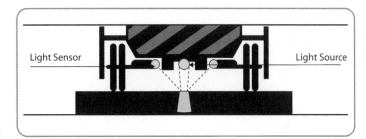

Figure 5.3 Light guidance system.

Sensors and feedback

Automated systems use sensors to pick up data and feed it back to the controlling computer. They use a wide range of sensors to detect things like heat, light, the presence of gas or smoke, pressure or weight, heat sensors, radiation.

How do sensors work?

A light sensor can be used to measure the amount of light in a room. The light hits the sensor and the sensor generates an electrical signal. The more light detected, the stronger the signal. When the signal varies continuously like

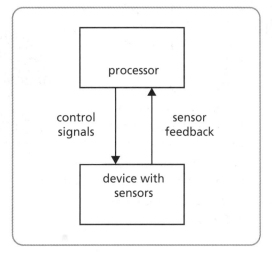

Figure 5.4 Block diagram showing feedback mechanisms.

this, it is known as an **analogue** signal. This **analogue** signal is then fed into the **interface**. The interface translates the **feedback** from the sensor into digital data that the processor can understand.

c Analogue input and output

The real world does not work in digital but in a range of analogue values. Digital devices must be able to handle analogue inputs and outputs if they are to work effectively.

Analogue to Digital Converter (ADC)

The type of interface used by to change the incoming **analogue** signals to **digital** data that can be understood by the processor is an **ADC.** It does this because, as you will remember from your system notes, the computer is only able to 'understand' **digital** data (binary using 0s and 1s).

Every second, the A to D chip in the interface takes thousands of samples of the incoming analogue signal, converts these samples into digital data and sends them to the processor.

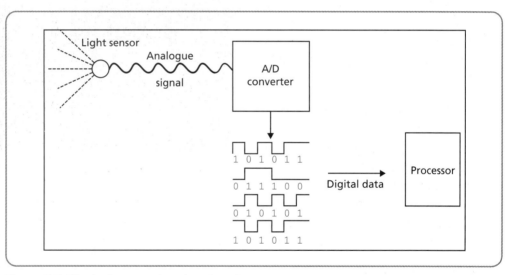

Figure 5.5 Block diagram showing A-to-D converter.

Digital to Analogue Converter (DAC)

A **DAC** reverses the process carried out by the **Analogue to Digital Converter** and converts the **digital** information from the processors into **analogue** signals. These are often used to control an electrical **motor** on a machine or robot arm.

Computer Aided Design (CAD)

Architects, engineers and planners use **CAD** systems for making complicated designs and plans of such as buildings, engine parts, cars and other manufactured items.

CAD workstations are equipped with a high-resolution monitor, a graphics pad, a powerful processor with lots of main memory and high capacity backing storage.

CAD systems are used because:

◆ designers can easily create objects/plans/designs in two or three dimensions and store them on backing store for use later;

◆ editing drawings is easy in CAD, as they can be altered, added to, deleted from, rotated and viewed from different angles;

◆ printing multiple copies is easier than having to draw them again by hand.

Computer Aided Manufacture (CAM)

CAM uses computer-controlled machines to make objects. The machines can be robot arms or lathes used for cutting shapes from metal. Once instructions are fed to them they will accurately cut the shape over and over again until told to stop.

Figure 5.6 Metal-working lathe.

In an integrated **CAD/CAM** system, an object is designed using a CAD system and the finished design is translated into a series of instructions that are transmitted to the CAM system that makes or assembles the designed object according to those instructions. This means that manufacturers can make changes to their products very quickly and with very little disruption to the manufacturing processes.

Safety procedures

Safety procedures are very important when automated systems are used in workplaces where people are moving about. The dangers are obvious – mobile robots can collide with people and fixed robots can cause injuries while moving their arms around. The types of safety precaution that can be taken include:

◆ reserving areas for the sole use of robots by hanging signs or painting markers on the floor;

◆ preventing everyone except qualified maintenance staff from approaching robots;

◆ fitting mobile robots with lights and sirens to warn people of their approach;

◆ using sensors to detect objects in the path of the robot (sound, heat or bump sensors could be used).

Questions

1. Why would an automated system be used in the following places?

   ◆ An oil refinery
   ◆ A factory making circuit boards for mobile phones
   ◆ A car factory

2. How does a magnetic guidance system for a mobile robot work?

3. Give an advantage of a light guidance system for a mobile robot.

4. Complete this table about the tools on robot arms in a car factory.

Tool	Use
Spray gun	painting
	picking up car windscreens
	welding

Simulation

Simulations can be used to train people and to help them develop skills such as driving a car or flying a plane by using a computer-based model. Simulators can be very realistic and accurate ways of training people to handle complex machinery in an environment where a learner's mistakes are not dangerous or costly.

A space shuttle simulation can be run a number of times, with the trainee pilot able to experience many different types of emergency without any risk to people or expensive equipment.

Figure 5.7 Flight simulator machine.

Virtual Reality (VR)

A **VR** system is an advanced form of simulation that can create the illusion that the user is part of the computer's world and can move about and manipulate that world.

In order for the system to react to the movements of the user it uses a range of specialised sensors that detect movement through magnetic fields. These are fitted to the gloves, suits and headsets worn by the user. The user can point to, lift and 'touch' objects in the virtual world.

The headset has a pair of small screens that create a 3-D visual effect. The feeling of reality is enhanced by sound from headphones to immerse the user in the world of the computer.

Virtual Reality systems can be used for:

Figure 5.8 Virtual reality helmet.

◆ training people to drive a car, fly a plane or run a nuclear reactor;

◆ creating a 3-D plan of a new construction which can be looked at from all angles – even from the inside! A plan of building or even a whole town can be simulated using a VR system;

◆ games and leisure activities – the sky is no limit in VR!

Real-time processing

A simulation must be realistic. One way for this to be achieved is to have the simulation running in **real-time**. Here the input signals are fed to the processor, which then checks the data and instantly responds to it. This is known as **real-time processing**.

This instant processing of data fed in by sensors is vital when automated systems are required to react to situations that can change very quickly. For example, an automated system that controls the flight path of a plane has to react instantly, for safety reasons.

What you need to know about controlling automated systems

Automated systems are controlled by computer programs. These programs contain high-level instructions telling the machine what to do. A program for a robot arm could contain instructions such as *left 30°*, *open gripper*, *forward 10*, *close gripper*.

Control language

The programs written to control a robot arm, or other automated system, are written in a dedicated **control language**. These languages have data types and control structures designed to help design software for controlling a particular machine.

ROM-based software

The instructions for controlling these systems are commonly stored in **ROM**. The software is part of the automated system and is built when the system is manufactured. This is good system design since the control software is in constant use and having it stored **permanently** in **ROM** avoids the need for loading from backing storage during startup.

Embedded systems

Many of the machines that we use have software built into them. These are called embedded systems and they appear in everything from mobile phones to car engines. These are small-scale computer systems, complete with their own processors and memory, built into the machine to enable it to carry out its functions. Many embedded systems have a simple control panel or touch screen to enable the user to select functions.

Intelligent robots

Intelligent robots have:

◆ powerful processors and large built-in memory;

◆ the ability to communicate with other computers and robots;

◆ a wide range of specialised sensors, such as optical or sonar sensors that enable them to find their way around objects;

◆ microphones and voice recognition systems to allow verbal input of commands.

Intelligent robots are capable of carrying out a wide range of sophisticated tasks like cleaning swimming pools, cutting the lawn, space exploration, playing table tennis. There has even been a robot world cup!

Questions

5. Give two reasons for using simulators

6. List three things a virtual reality system can be used for.

7. Why do the computers on board an aircraft use real-time processing?

Credit

8. What is a control language used for?

9. Why is ROM based software used?

10. Give an example of an embedded system.

11. Describe two ways in which an intelligent robot is different from an ordinary robot.

Social, technical and economic implications

The widespread use of automated systems in industry has a range of implications for the ways people work and the ways businesses are run and manufacture their products.

Social implications

Changing working practices

In the manufacturing industries, many of the skilled jobs operating machines have been taken over by computer-controlled machines. This process of modernisation has allowed manufacturing to cut costs and reduce wastage. This has led to lower prices and increased competition. Without this shift, many firms would have gone out of business, undercut by those manufacturers who have automated their businesses.

This change has meant that the jobs that people do have changed. The work is less physically demanding and less dangerous. People have more leisure time. Some skilled jobs have almost gone, taken over by machines, but other jobs have been created in the support services for those machines.

New types of jobs

◆ The types of jobs that people **are** needed for are:

◆ maintenance of machines and computer hardware;

◆ installation, maintenance and updating of software;

◆ managerial, supervisory and quality control tasks.

Retraining

Some people might have to go on training courses so that they can do these new jobs and fit in with the automated systems.

Economic implications

Initial costs

A lot of money has to be invested when setting up an automated system to pay for:

◆ the systems analyst to design the new system;

◆ building or refitting the factory and office to suit the new machines;

◆ buying and installing the robots, computer hardware and new software;

◆ training programs for the staff.

Replacement costs

Equipment needs to be repaired or upgraded regularly. This can apply to all the parts of an automated system from the processors to the mobile and stationary robots. Replacement costs can be quite high and need to be built into the business plan of any organisation using automated systems.

Long term savings

Businesses are prepared to meet the high initial costs and the running costs, because in the long term their overall costs are reduced.

As we saw at the start of this chapter, automated systems work faster and can handle repetitive work with fewer mistakes than any human operator. This makes them much more efficient than traditional systems. Costs are cut by reducing wage bills, by increasing the amount of goods produced and by cutting out waste.

Key points about the design of a factory using automated systems

Designing the layout of a new factory means looking at:

◆ where the robot arms should go;

◆ creating paths for the mobile robots;

◆ communications with the automated systems using cables or a wireless system;

◆ safety procedures.

What you need to know about the job of the systems analyst

When designing a new factory a systems analyst has to:

◆ map out all the tasks that are carried out in the production of a car (for example);

◆ analyse how these tasks are related to each other;

◆ decide which type of automated system is needed for each of these tasks;

◆ recommend a design for the physical layout of the factory.

The systems analyst needs to know:

◆ how many robot arms are needed;

◆ where they should be situated;

◆ how many mobile robots are needed;

◆ whether to use a magnetic or light guidance system for the mobile robots;

◆ the types of sensors needed and where are they should be located;

◆ the type of computer needed to control the system.

Questions

12. List two new types of jobs that an automated system can create.

13. Describe two initial costs.

14. Why do businesses pay the expensive initial costs?

15. Give an example of a replacement cost.

Credit

16. List four things a systems analyst has to do when designing a new factory.

PROBLEM SOLVING

Get your problem solving up to speed! Answer these problem solving questions!
Have fun.

1. The hospital managers have decided to introduce a new computer system to
   deal with patients' records. The software package is quite easy to use.

   a) What kind of HCI do you think it has?

   b) Copy and complete this table by choosing the correct word from this list:
      wizard, word wrap, template, toolbar, menu

Which feature will help the nurses by stepping them through a complicated task?	
Which feature will help the nurses to speed up making documents by setting out the styles, margins and headings in advance?	
Which feature helps the user by having all the things they can do on the package set out as a row of icons.	

   c) As a result of introducing a computer system into the hospital, many of the
      staff will need to be trained. After they have been on the training course
      they will need some sort of help. State 2 ways the software could help them.

   d) The hospital administrator would like to keep all their records on computer
      and be able to find patients records quickly. What type of package would
      you suggest they keep their records on? Give reasons for your choice.

   e) Which package would you use to produce the letters that will be sent to
      patients?

   f) List 2 features of that package that will be useful to them in producing the
      letters.

   g) The hospital staff want to produce a slide show of the hospital to help train
      new staff.

      (i) Which package should they use to produce the slide show?

      (ii) List 4 features of that package that would help them to produce the
           slide show.

   h) (i) The managers want the software to be able to produce monthly reports.
           These reports will combine text, graphics and lists of numbers and totals.
           What type of package should they use?

(ii) It is suggested that it would be a good idea if the software had a common HCI. How would a common HCI make it easier to use the software?

i) (i) The staff will need to produce graphs of the patients that pass through the hospital each month. Which part of the package will they use to produce the graph?

(ii) Once the first graph has been produced the staff decide they need to add the title **Outpatients Department** to the spreadsheet and graph. Explain how setting up a dynamic link would help them do this.

2 The Eagle Insurance company decides to set up a web page to publicise the company.

a) Name two types of data could they include in the website to make it as attractive as possible to people.

b) What would they use to join the web pages together and help people move about the website?

c) The graphics and text on the web pages are difficult to control. They never seem to stay together. What can the designers do to fix this?

d) What can they do to make the web pages more interactive and to let people select more information on objects shown on a web page?

3 Eagle Insurance salesmen use a spreadsheet to keep track of the amount of money they make by selling insurance policies.

a) Copy and complete this table by choosing the correct word from this list:

MIN, relative referencing, IF, labelling, AVERAGE, cell protection, SUM, absolute referencing, MAX.

Which spreadsheet function should they use to find the customer that owes the most money?	
Which function should they use to find the customer that owes the least money?	
How can they stop the contents of a cell being changed accidentally?	

Which type of formula should they use to give a rebate to those customers who pay more than £100 per month.	
The salesmen want to copy and paste a formula around the spreadsheet yet still have it lock onto a cell which holds the interest rate. What can they use to do this?	
The salesmen want to copy and paste a formula around the spreadsheet which will vary according to the cell it is moved to. What can they use to do this?	
People have said that the graphs that the salesmen produce are very hard to understand. What feature can be used to make the graphs easier to understand?	

b) How would an expert system help the Insurance Company make predictions?

4 Calum is writing a program which must be able to run on several very different computer systems.

a) What kind of programming language must he use? Give a reason.

b) As he writes his program the data is entered in RAM memory. What does he need to do before he switches off in order to make sure he can load the program next time he is on the computer?

c) Calum organises his files by putting them into _____.

d) The part of the computer system he uses to do this is called the _____.

e) Calum has too many folders on his hard disk. It is difficult to find anything. How can he improve the organisation of these folders?

f) Calum's High Level Language program is translated into machine code using a compiler. Give two reasons for using a compiler.

5 An insurance company wants a mainframe to be installed which will allow it to handle requests for data from its offices throughout Scotland and, at the same time, be able to produce customer statements in between data requests from the offices. One analyst suggests installing 2 separate systems each with a different type of operating system. Can you think of an alternative, better, solution to this problem?

6 The bank manager finds that the desktop computer he uses is a bit too slow. You suggest buying a machine with a bigger word size. How would this make his computer work a bit quicker?

7 Your teacher asks you to design a computer system to help deliver courses to Standard Grade classes. The materials on the courses will take the form of:

◆ text based information sheets;

◆ diagrams and still photos;

◆ video clips;

◆ sound clips.

What kind of system would you recommend?

8 An electronics factory, Electrosound, makes MP3 players using an automated production line with mobile and stationary robots.

a) Which type of processing is necessary to make the robots work efficiently. Interactive processing or real-time processing? Give reasons for your answer.

b) The business uses robots because they are adaptable. What is it that makes them adaptable?

c) The software controlling the robots is written using a control language. Why is this necessary?

d) The mobile robots have the controlling software stored on ROM chips. What advantage does this have?

e) The factory considers using intelligent robots. Describe two ways in which they are different from ordinary robots.

Answers

(?)

1. a) A GUI, probably a WIMP

b)

This will help the nurses by stepping them through a complicated task	wizard
The nurses can use this to speed up making documents by setting out the styles, margins and headings in advance	template
This helps the user by having all the things they can do on the package set out as a row of icons.	toolbar

c) On-line help, on-line tutorial

d) Database because it is designed to hold records in files and to enable users to search and sort the data.

e) Word processing package.

f) Search and replace, spell check, grammar check, standard paragraphs etc.

g) i) Presentation package or a multimedia authoring package.

ii) Templates, hyperlinks, wizards, ability to add graphics, sound and video

h) i) An integrated package

ii) People would not need to learn new icons, menus or commands for each application because they would all be similar.

i) i) The spreadsheet application will have a charting facility.

ii) A dynamic link means that when the spreadsheet is amended the changes will show up automatically in the chart.

2. a) video, still graphics, sound

b) hyperlinks

c) Use tables in the web pages to control the position of text and graphics.

d) Use hotspots.

3. a)

Which function should they use to find the customer that owes the most money?	MAX
Which function should they use to find the customer that owes the least money?	MIN
How can they stop the contents of a cell being changed accidentally?	Use cell protection and lock the cell.
Which type of formula should they use to give a rebate to those customers who pay more than £100 per month.	**IF** formula.
The salesmen want to copy and paste a formula around the spreadsheet yet still have it lock onto a cell which holds the interest rate. What can they use to do this?	Absolute referencing
The salesmen want to copy and paste a formula around the spreadsheet which will vary according to the cell it is moved to. What can they use to do this?	Relative referencing
People have said that the charts (graphs) that the salesmen produce are very hard to understand. What can they do to improve this?	They need to make sure that the charts are fully labelled.

b) It would hold all the knowledge of an expert and make it available to all their salesmen to help them make decisions and give customers expert advice.

4. a) A high level language, because the program will be portable.

b) He needs to save it to backing storage e.g. his hard disk.

c) Calum organises his files by putting them into directories.

d) The part of the computer system he uses to do this is called the operating system.

e) By organising them into hierarchical directories.

f) It does not need the translator loaded into memory and using processor time when the program is running. It only does the translation once and then saves the machine code.

5. An interactive operating system with background processing capability.

6. The larger the word size the more data the processor can manipulate in any one operation.

7. A multimedia system.

8. a) Real time processing because the processor checks the data and responds to it instantly, which is vital when controlling machinery.

   b) They can be re-programmed. Robot arms can have different tools fitted for different tasks.

   c) Control languages have data types and control structures designed to help design software for controlling a particular machine.

   d) Control software is in constant use and having it stored permanently in ROM avoids the need for loading from backing storage during startup.

   e) They have powerful processors and large built-in memory; they have the ability to communicate with other computers and robots; They have sensors which enable them to mimic human senses such as sight and hearing.

FOCUS ON THE EXTERNAL EXAMINATION

The importance of your practical work

The Standard Grade exam is worth 60% of your overall grade. The other 40% comes from the practical work you have done in class and will be completed well before you sit the exam. Make sure you work very hard at your practical tasks as they do count towards your final grade. Your teacher will tell you what your grade is for your practical work.

Know your topics, solve your problems

In the written exam there will be questions which check your knowledge and understanding of the topics in the course. There will also be questions on problem solving. In the exam, marks gained in the Problem Solving section are worth double the marks gained in the Knowledge and Understanding section. This means that problem solving is very important and getting good marks for problem solving makes it easier to get a good overall grade. Make sure you have completed the problem solving questions in this book!

Two exam papers

You will sit two exam papers: either Foundation and General or General and Credit. Your teacher will tell you which ones you need to prepare for. If you are sitting General and Credit you will need to know all the topics in this book and to answer all the questions! If you are sitting Foundation and General papers you can skip the sections marked as credit and you don't need to answer the Credit questions. All the Credit topics and questions are marked in this book by the Credit icon Ⓒ.

Exam preparation tips

◆ Draw up a revision plan well before the exam, scheduling your revision so that you can cover it all without leaving it to the last minute.

◆ Use a checklist to make sure you cover all the topics.

◆ Learn the definitions of all the topics in this book.

◆ Check your knowledge is up to exam standard by answering all the questions in this book.

◆ Make sure you complete all the Problem Solving questions in this book and check the answers.

◆ Answer the following exam style practice questions, then check the answers.

Exam style practice questions

Foundation level

1 Pupils at Dunwearie High School are selling cakes at lunchtime to raise money for a trip to Bolivia. Below is a spreadsheet containing the money taken in one day.

	A	B	C	D
1	The Bolivia Experience			
2				
3	Cake	Price Each	Number Sold	Total
4	Angel Cake	0.20	45	9.00
5	Coconut Slice	0.20	39	7.80
6	Chocolate Fudge Bro	0.15	94	14.10
7	Jam Tart	0.10	57	5.70
8	Rock Bun	0.15	48	7.20
9	Shortbread	0.10	104	10.40
10		Totals	387	54.20

a) Complete the following sentences using the words:

   cell   column   row

   i) The text 'Jam Tart' is held in _____ **A7**.

   ii) The price of each cake is held in _____ **B**.

   iii) The information about Rock Buns is held in _____ **8**.

b) Write down the formula used to calculate the total money collected by selling **Angel Cakes**.

   = _____

c) The total number of cakes sold that day was **387**. Write down the formula used to calculate this total.

   = _____

d) The name 'Chocolate Fudge Brownie' is not displayed properly. What is the name of the feature of spreadsheets that will allow the whole name to be shown.

   _____

e) 'Marshmallow cakes' have been missed out. What is the name of the feature of spreadsheets that will allow this to be added to the list

_____

2 Sophina has just bought a new internet-ready computer. It has a modem installed and comes with the latest operating system.

a) Use arrows to connect the four boxes in the following diagram of a simple computer system.

| Input |

| Processor |
| RAM | ROM |

| Output |

| Backing Storage |

b) What is an operating system?

_____

c) The operating system comes with a browser. What is a browser?

_____

d) The two types of main memory are RAM and ROM. What does **ROM** stand for?

R_____ O_____ M_____

e) Sophina wants to send an e-mail to her friend in Birmingham. Describe two advantages of using e-mail instead of sending a letter.

1_____

2_____

General Questions

1 Pupils at Dunwearie High School are selling cakes at lunchtime to raise money for a trip to Bolivia. Below is a spreadsheet containing the money taken in one day. The cakes are in alphabetical order.

	A	B	C	D
1	The Bolivia Experience			
2				
3	Cake	Price Each	Number Sold	Total
4	Angel Cake	0.20	45	9.00
5	Coconut Slice	0.20	39	7.80
6	Chocolate Fudge Bro	0.15	94	14.10
7	Jam Tart	0.10	57	5.70
8	Rock Bun	0.15	48	7.20
9	Shortbread	0.10	104	10.40
10		Totals	387	54.20

a) The formulae used in column **D** were **not** typed in individually. Name the spreadsheet feature that has been used to achieve this.

_____

_____

b) The pupils want to include a formula in cell **D11** to calculate the largest amount of money made by a single type of cake. Write down the formula used in cell **D11**.

= _____

c) The total amount of money taken that day was **54.20**, but when the cell is selected it shows **54.2**. Describe what has been done to the cell to make it display **54.20**

_____

_____

d) After the spreadsheet was typed in, the pupils wanted to make sure that the formulae were not accidentally changed. Describe how this could have been done.

_____

_____

e) When setting up the spreadsheet, the pupils did not know how to change how columns **B** and **D** look. Name the feature of the spreadsheet that they used to find out how this could be done.

_____

_____

2 Ruth has just connected her computer to the Local Area Network (LAN) at her work. This allows her to pass messages or files to her fellow workers and to view web pages.

a) State two methods of protecting her files from unauthorised access by other users of the LAN.

_____

_____

b) The web pages are written in HTML. What does **HTML** stand for?

H _____ **T** _____ **M** _____ **L** _____

c) Ruth uses a search engine frequently. What is a **search engine**?

_____

_____

d) Ruth has just completed a twelve-page report about backing storage devices, but she realises that she has written 'USB drive' instead of 'USB flash drive' throughout the document. Describe how she could use a feature of her word processor to correct her error quickly.

_____

_____

_____

_____

e) Ruth receives an email from a friend, but it has several spelling errors in it. Her friend says that she used a spell checker on it before sending so it should have been correct. Give an example of **two** different types of error that the spell checker could have missed.

1 _____

_____

2 _____

_____

Credit Questions

1 Teachers at Dunwearie High School use a database to hold information on pupil tests. Part of the information held is shown below

Forename	Surname	Class	Test 1	Test 2	Test 3	Final Mark
Derek	Wilson	3M2	17	29	23	69
John	Harper	3L1	13	26	28	67
Kerry	Mathews	3E3	19	28	24	71
Stuart	Chalmers	3M1	20	27	29	76
Ken	Rodgers	3L3	18	25	27	70

a) i) State the field type of the 'Final Mark' field.

_____

ii) Describe how you would create the 'Final Mark' field in a database package with which you are familiar.

_____

_____

_____

_____

_____

b) A search was carried out on the database to find those pupils in the year that scored more than 65 as their Final Mark. A standard letter will be sent out to their parents praising their achievement. State the feature of the word processor that could be used to produce the 32 standard letters quickly.

_____

_____

_____

c) i) The Head Teacher of Dunwearie High School is named as the data controller for the above database. Name the Act of Parliament that defines a 'data controller'.

_____

ii) What is the name given to the pupils in the database by this Act?

_____

d) Some of the information in the database is to be sent to the SQA. It is copied from the database and saved in an RTF file. This file is then sent by email.

i) What does 'RTF' stand for?

_____

ii) Describe one advantage of sending the data in this format.

_____

2 Abby has just bought a new computer and laser printer. The computer has the latest processor and operating system.

a) The processor has three main parts: registers, the Control Unit and the Arithmetic/Logic Unit (ALU). Describe the function of the following parts:

i) Control Unit:

_____

_____

ii) ALU:

_____

_____

b) The operating system has many parts. Describe the function of the memory management system.

_____

_____

_____

_____

c) When Abby connects her printer to the new computer it will not print. The error message says that there is a software problem. What is likely to be causing the error?

_____

_____

_____

_____

d) Abby sends a graphic file as an e-mail attachment to another member of her team. The file contains a black and white line drawing. The file is 1600 by 1200 pixels. Calculate the file size of the graphic. Show all of your working. Your answer should be in appropriate units.

_____

_____

_____

_____

_____

_____

e) Abby downloads some anti-virus software for her new computer. This software is shareware. After ten days she gets a message saying that her software is now illegal and tells her to do one of two things. Describe the two ways that that she can solve her problem.

1 _____

2 _____

Answers to Foundation questions

Answers and marking instructions

1 a i) The text 'Jam Tart' is held in **cell** A7.

   ii) The price of each cake is held in **column** B.

   iii) The information about Rock Buns is held in **row** 8.
       (1 mark for each correct answer)

   b =B4*C4
      (1 mark for ***** for the multiplication symbol, 1 mark for both cell references correct)

   c = SUM(C4:C9)
      (1 mark for SUM function, 1 mark for correct range). Note: Accept other valid syntax including correct use of comma. Do not accept simple addition.

   d Change column width.
      (1 mark) Accept 'Column width'

   e Insert row.
      (1 mark)

2 a Arrows need to be added to the diagram as shown here:

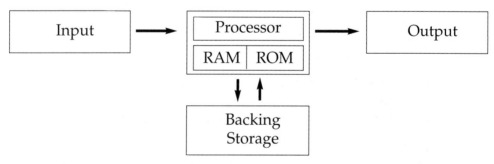

   (1 mark for each arrow, maximum 3)

   Accept a double-headed arrow for Backing Storage connection

   b A set of (systems) programs to control the (operation of the) computer.
      (1 mark for valid answer)

   c Software to look at web pages
      (1 mark) Do not accept 'to look for web pages'

   d Read Only Memory
      (2 marks for all three correct, 1 mark for any two)

e Any two from the following list for 1 mark each, max 2:

She does not need to walk to the post box
An e-mail does not cost as much (or is free) to send
Her friend will get the message faster
Sophina will get a reply faster
Her friend can pick up the email anywhere
Any other valid

Note: Both answers must be complete descriptions (not single words 'faster' etc) and they must be sufficiently different answers.

Answers to General questions

Answers and marking instructions

1 a Replication/Fill Down
(1 mark)
Note: Do not accept 'Fill' without direction. 'Copy/Paste' may be accepted by SQA Markers but is not guaranteed!

b =MAX(D4:D9)
(1 mark for MAX – accept 'MAXIMUM', 1 mark for correct range)

c ◆ Cell/number attributes/format
◆ Set/fixed to 2 decimal places
(1 mark for each bullet point)

d ◆ Select cells with formulae
◆ Choose cell protection
(1 mark for each bullet point, accept valid alternatives)

e On-line Help
(1 mark)

2 a Any two from the following list for 1 mark each, max 2 marks

Encryption/encoding of data
Password protect files
Set user access rights/hierarchical access to network
Any other valid
Note: Purely physical methods are not appropriate here

b Hyper Text Markup Language
(1 mark for each two words correct)

c Software to look for web pages on a specific topic

It will find a range of web pages related to words entered by Ruth

(1 mark) Do not accept simply 'to look for web pages'

d She could use the Find and Replace feature to find the phrase 'USB drive' and replace it with 'USB flash drive'. (1 mark)

e Any two from the following list for 1 mark each, max 2 marks.

Grammar errors (word order, punctuation, etc)
Mistyped words that are words themselves (the/then, her/here)
Wrong word used (two/too/to, ware/where/wear)

Note: Both answers must include examples and they must be sufficiently different answers (not ewe/you and witch/which).

Answers to Credit questions

Answers and marking instructions

1 a i) Computed/Calculated/Calculation field (1 mark)

ii) ◆ Go to 'define fields' (or equivalent) and created a computed field

◆ Enter calculation as 'Test 1 + Test 2 + Test 3'

(1 mark for each bullet point, accept valid alternatives)

b Mail Merge (1 mark)

c i) Data Protection Act (1 mark)

ii) Data subject(s) (1 mark)

Do not accept 'subjects' alone

d i) Rich Text Format (1 mark)

ii) Data can be read by any package (1 mark)

2 a i) The Control Unit:

◆ controls the operation of the processor

- ◆ controls the flow of data and instructions round the processor

- ◆ any other valid

(1 mark for any one bullet)

ii) ALU performs the logical and arithmetic calculations (1 mark)

b Organises the use of RAM

Allocates RAM to files and programs
Ensures that there is enough space for programs before loading
(1 mark)

Note that answers like 'manages memory/RAM' are insufficient

c She does not have the correct printer driver (1 mark)

d 1 mark for each stage of calculation, max 3 marks.

$1600 \times 1200 = 1920\,000$ pixels
$1920\,000/8 = 240\,000$ bytes (accept 1920 000 bits)
$240\,000/1024 = 234.375 = 234$ Kilobytes

e 1 mark for each bullet point:
- ◆ delete the expired shareware
- ◆ pay the shareware fee

FOCUS ON THE EXTERNAL EXAMINATION

ANSWERS

Chapter 1

General Purpose Packages

1. audio: music file like an MP3;
   video: a file holding a movie on your DVD;
   animation: an animated piece of clipart GIF;
   photographic: the jpeg from your digital camera.

2. It's a copy made in case a file is lost or corrupted.

3. This one's for you: check your files on your system.

4. Because they contain series of graphics that are displayed one after another.

5. You need to work out how long the movie is and then calculate how many frames it holds. A movie that is one hour long has $60 \times 60 \times 25$ frames = 90 000 frames, or 90 000 Megabytes (90 Gigabytes). In compressed form, this would reduce to 1.8 Gigabytes.

6. Advantage: the file is saved with all its formatting intact.

7. **Window**: an area on the screen displaying an application or a document.
   Icon: a graphic representing a file, a printer, a GPP.
   Menu: displays a range of options for the user to choose from
   Pointer: used to select from a menu

8. It would be very difficult, awkward to use.

9. A GUI is a type of HCI in which icons and on-screen graphics to control a package.

10. On-line tutorial and on-line help.

11. Toolbar is a type of menu with a set of icons for tasks that are carried out frequently. This saves the user from having to look through lots of menus

12. Templates are documents with the structure and much of the formatting already in place.

13. A wizard is a piece of software that guides you step by step through a complicated process.

14. Any two of: changing the size of the icons, the background colour of your desktop, the speed of the pointer.

15. They help get things done quicker, without having to go through a series of menus.

16. a) Because it has all the different types of application needed for the task and it makes it easy to swap data between them.

    b) Statistics and graphs = spreadsheet, written report = word processing.

    c) Open the window with the spreadsheet data and copy and paste it into the window in the word processing package which holds the text.

    d) Because the teacher won't have to learn how to use a completely new set of menus and icons for each part of the integrated package.

    e) Dynamic linkage, because if the numbers in the spreadsheet are changed later on it will update the integrated document automatically.

    f) The integrated suite will have more functionality. It will have many more features available to the user. Disadvantage: it will cost more and it will need more space on backing storage and main memory.

17. **Word-wrap**: When a word is too long to fit at the end of a line the application automatically moves the whole word onto the next line.
    Standard paragraph: A paragraph of text that is already typed in, checked and saved. It can be inserted directly into a document, saving time.
    Text style: Making text **bold**, *italics* or underlined.
    Find and replace: The user enters a word or phrase and the package looks for it and replaces it with another one.
    Grammar check: This checks that the text follows the rules of the English language. If a grammar rule has been broken it may offer suggestions to help improve the text.
    Table: Tables are set out in rows and columns and are used to organise text layout.
    Page break: Forces a new page.
    Standard letter: A letter which is sent to many different people. It is stored on disk and is automatically called up and personalised by having details added such as date, names and addresses.
    Mail merge: The automated process of personalising standard letters by taking names and addresses etc from a database or table, entering them on the standard letter then sending them to the printer.

18. **Row**: A horizontal line of cells in a spreadsheet.
    Column: A vertical line of cells in a spreadsheet.
    Cell: Single location within a spreadsheet.
    Formula: A calculation using numbers, other cells or even text. *Simple* formulae might use one or two mathematical symbols (+ - / *).
    SUM function: This function adds up the cells in the range entered by the user.
    Automatic calculation: with the Automatic Calculation facility on, the spreadsheet will automatically recalculate all the formulae if any changes are made to the data.
    Simple charting: Make a chart (graph) from spreadsheet data.
    Complex formula: A formula with more than one element to it such as
    =((A4+B4)/ (C8-16))* (D6+D7)
    AVERAGE function: Calculates the average in the range of cells entered by the user.
    MINIMUM function: Calculates the smallest value in the range of cells entered by the user.
    MAXIMUM function: Calculates the largest value in the range of cells entered by the user.
    Replicate: A feature which copies a formula across a row or down a column
    Cell attributes: The display characteristics of a cell such as setting the number of decimal places to be shown.
    Cell protection: This facility is for protecting the contents of cells that you do not want to be accidentally changed or deleted.

19. IF(condition,true,false)

20. Absolute reference is used to make sure that, wherever in a spreadsheet it is copied to, a formula always refers back to the same cell. The cell with the absolute reference is indicated by using a $. Relative reference is used when the cells a formula is referencing need to change as it is copied across a row or down a column.

21 **File**: A set of records
   Record: A set of fields
   Field: Holds an item of data
   Alter record format: Change the structure of a record, by changing the number of fields, length of fields or type of fields.
   Search, query or **find on one field:** Search for those records where the first_name field = 'Jack'
   Sort on one field: Sort on the Second_name field

Search on **more than one field:** . search for those records where the first_name field = 'Jean' AND the second_name field = 'Brown'

Sort on **more than one field**: Sort on grade field and on the name field.

Keyword: A word or phrase or number that is used to make searching a database easier e.g. exam candidate number.

Altering the screen output format: To change the arrangement of fields and records as they are displayed and/or printed out.

Altering the screen input format: To change the arrangement of the data fields and their field names in a data entry form which is displayed on screen e.g. from card to column format.

22. **Tool attributes**: The properties of a tool or object such as the thickness, colour or pattern of a line.

Scale graphic: Change the dimensions of a graphic by altering its height or width.

Rotate graphic: Turn a graphic around to view it from another angle by dragging the graphic using the mouse and cursor, or by entering the number of degrees through which the graphic will turn.

Crop graphic: Cut out an area of a graphic and keep the rest.

Scan graphic: To capture a picture for use on the computer using a scanner.

Edit graphic: To make changes to a graphic once it has been scanned or inserted.

23. **Template**: Documents with most of the formatting and layout already set up such as the fonts, sizes, text and graphic frames and colours.

Slides with linear links: Slides together automatically so that they follow one after another.

Import graphic: Bring a graphic file from a graphics package, clip art, digital photograph, or the Internet into a DTP or presentation package.

Import text: DTP packages enable you to set up a *text frame* and bring in your text from a word processing document.

Change layout: Altering the position of text frames and graphic objects using the precise control which comes with desktop publishing applications.

Text wrap around graphics: Enables you to let your text flow around a graphic.

24. Hyperlinks

25. To enable the user to take different paths through the website or slide show.

26. They would enable you to control the position of your graphics and text and hyperlinks.

27. They add interactivity so that they let the user interact with the page.

28. To help the user solve problems in a specific subject area by storing and using the knowledge of one or more experts in that subject.

29. A group of experts in a subject set down all the facts and rules that apply to the system. These rules and facts are checked and then entered into an expert system.

30. Medicine, banking and finance, geology, network diagnostics.

31. They hold all the knowledge of an expert in a software application. They support people when they have to make decisions by providing expert advice when no human expert is available. The knowledge is not lost if the experts are ill or die.

32. a) Word processor

    b) Graphics package

    c) DTP

    d) Presentation

    e) Database

    f) Spreadsheet

    g) Multimedia/Presentation

    h) Expert system

33. Because they need to learn how to use the new hardware and software.

34. No. Information that is held on police computers is not covered by the Data Protection Act.

35. Paying for computer hardware, software or a systems analyst.

36. Replacing monitors, hard disks, keyboards, etc.

37. Telecoms bill, electricity.

38. Staff wages

39. Not necessarily, the availability of printers can mean a lot more documents are easily available.

40. IDs and passwords.

41. A hacker.

42. Data subject: individual to whom data relates;

Data controller: the person, business or organisation who controls the collection and use of personal data;
Data user: an individual in an organisation who makes use of personal data.

43. Any from any of the following:
    ◆ data is processed only if the consent of the individual is given;
    ◆ if it is part of a legal contract;
    ◆ if it is essential to a business transaction or the carrying out of public duties;
    ◆ it must be held for the specified purposes described in the Register entry.

44. Interfering with a system so that it doesn't run properly, making changes to the system to prevent others accessing the system, making changes to the software or data.

45. Making unauthorised (pirate) copies of software, running pirate software, transmitting software over telecommunications links and copying it, running multiple copies of software if only one copy was purchased, giving lending or selling copies of bought software unless license to do so is granted

Chapter 2

Communications and networks

1. Any two of: share peripherals such as hard drives and printers, share data and programs, work on shared projects, communicate by sending e-mails, backup data more effectively, control security more effectively.

2. Advantages: they are easy to install, as there is no need for cables. You can move around when you work without trailing wires. Disadvantage: vulnerable to hackers, who can just 'tap in' to your signal.

3. It is a network which can link computers across towns, countries and around the world.

4. Physical: security locks on the doors and windows of computer rooms, locks on workstations themselves, no removable backing storage available, such as floppy drives.

System: unique network IDs and passwords, encryption password protection for individual files, multi-level access rights, biometric systems.

5. To connect a computer to a LAN.

6. A computer where many users can share the computer's resources at the one time.

7. Print, file, application, mail, web servers.

8. Mobile phones, or PCs, are used to send short messages, text or picture, to other users.

9. Speed of delivery compared with surface mail, low cost compared with surface mail, you can sent attachments, documents or pictures, around the world, ability to check mail from any network workstation or Internet connection, security: mail is protected by IDs and passwords, ability to send multiple copies of mail at the one time, ability to store and organise messages.

10. Netiquette is a code of conduct, or set of rules, to guide behaviour when using email or a network e.g. do not send spam, be polite, do not use capital letters, it is considered to be SHOUTING.

11. Dial-up: uses an ordinary phone line and a modem to dial up and connect a computer to the Internet. It has a bandwidth, speed, of 56 kilobits per second (kbps). Broadband connection: a high-speed telecommunications link that works 10+ times faster than a dial-up connection. The standard bandwidths for this type of connection are from 0.5 megabit per second (mbps) to 2 mbps.

12. Because it can send and receive data so much faster.

13. It is made up of multimedia web pages that are stored on computers across the world. Web pages hold text, sounds, graphics, animations, and videos. These are linked together by hyperlinks.

14. She needs to set up a series of hyperlinks.

15. It is a page description language which uses tags or commands to set up the headings, colours, graphics and text that make up a Web page.

Credit questions

16. A 'smartphone': one with browser and Internet access.

17. Send it as an attachment.

18. By using a complex search with two or more conditions in it. In this case 'loch', 'Scotland' and 'Fort William'.

19. It could use shareware, giving users a 30 day free trial and allowing them to copy and pass it on to others.

20. Businesses often have special offers only available on their website and some companies only advertise jobs on the web.

Chapter 3

Computer systems

1. Because all programs written in a high level language need to be translated into machine code before the instructions can be carried out by the system.

2. Because HLL are very similar to English and so are easier to use.

3. Because it is only translated once and then the machine code version is ready to run.

4. It is portable if it can be run on a system other than the one on which it was written with little or no change.

5. Any system that reacts instantly to data is called real time e.g. in aircraft control systems.

6. Program files are the programs and applications that the system runs, like MS Word or HALO. Data files contain information used by the program files.

7. Any two of: providing the Human Computer Interface (HCI) for the user, file management, memory management, error reporting.

8. The system starts at the beginning of the data sequence and reads each piece of data until it locates what it needs.

9. The file management system manages the loading and saving of files. It involves carrying out tasks such as creating and deleting files, organising files into directories and sub-directories, controlling access to files and locking files so they can't be changed.

10. Any two of: more orderly structure, allowing user to find data quicker, allows user to control access to directories

11. The processor is the 'brains' of the computer that deals with all the movement of data and any calculations to be carried out.

12. All data in RAM is lost when the power is switched off, data in ROM is not lost

when the power is switched off. Data held in RAM can be changed, while data held in ROM cannot be changed.

13. It is used to represent text.

14. Number of pixels = 48 sq inches × 300 × 300 = 4320000 bits = 540000 bytes = 527.3 Kilobytes.

15. Two of: powerful processors, large internal memory capacity and access to backing storage media which can store large volumes of data.

16. Two of: for storing and retrieving data, keeping a diary of appointments, as an MP3 player, communicating with a network.

17. Because they are more convenient to use than a mouse when you are travelling with the laptop.

18. To input freehand drawings into the computer.

19. Two of: they can hold lots of images without film, you can delete the pictures you don't want, you can transfer them to a computer and print them out.

20. For advertising business, for checking on traffic flows

21. Biosensors are used to detect movements in muscles and eyes. A mouse you can control by moving your head.

22. By taking tens of thousands of samples of the analogue sound waves each second, then changing each sample into a binary number and store each sample in memory.

23. Advantage: it produces high quality printouts. Disadvantage: it is more expensive to buy than an inkjet.

24. Their running costs, i.e. the cost of cartridges, are high and they are comparatively slow.

25. In dots per inch.

26. It has more complex electronics and can display graphics much more clearly.

27. A DVD-ROM holds between 4.7 and 17 Gigabytes of data. A CD-ROM holds 650 Megabytes.

28. Storing video files.

29. This is a small portable backing storage device, with no moving parts, which can store large amounts of data.

30. To relieve the main system memory and processor of the burden of storing and processing graphic data.

31. Stereo screens and stereo headphones, often built into a headset.

32. Tape drives

33. A method by which the system accesses data one block after another, in sequence.

Chapter 4

Commercial Data processing

1. a) a bank.

   b) because the data is stored on the cheque using special magnetic ink.

2. Recording simple responses e.g. numbers on a lottery card or a questionnaire.

3. The data on them is scanned into the system in a fraction of a second.

4. a) Most common way is to have on-screen verification where the operator has to check the data shown on screen.

   b) range check, field type check, presence check, field length check, check digit.

5. In case data is lost or corrupted.

6. Because it is important to update the files that hold the holiday bookings immediately.

7. Any three of: controlling access to the system, setting up user accounts, issuing IDs and passwords, controlling access to files by setting permissions, checking that any new software and hardware are compatible with the existing system before installing them on the network.

8. Deciding which tasks the system has to carry out, defining types of data needed and the processes to be carried out on that data, noting the information needed by the business / organisation.

9. Trading of goods and services on-line, using computer networks, is known as e-commerce.

10. Electronic Funds Transfer: the use of computer systems to transfer money between bank accounts.

11. Checking your balance, apply for a new account, order a cheque book, set up a standing order.

12. Advantages for **customer**: You can browse for goods 24/7, you can order and pay for goods without having to leave the house, many stores pass on some of the cost savings by offering special online deals.

    Advantages for **business**: keeps costs to a minimum as there is no need to pay for shops or wages, by using the Internet they can sell to a mass market, even worldwide, online payment means instant cash flow without the need to process cheques or cash.

13. Initial costs: wages of systems analysts, programmers and engineers, training costs for staff on the new system, cost of the actual hardware and software, purchase of suitable furniture.

    Running costs: staff wages, power and telecommunications costs, consumables such as: printer paper and toner, cost of maintaining the hardware and software.

14. It is a database which many people can access at the same time.

15. Because it enables data to be viewed and used by a whole range of people once it has been entered and stored centrally in the system.

Chapter 5

Automated Systems

1. An oil refinery would use an automated system to monitor pressures, gases basically to run a complex alarm system.

   A factory making circuit boards would use an automated system to place components on the circuit boards accurately, at high speed.

   Car factories use automated systems to weld, to spray paint, to carry materials, to install windscreens.

2. Magnetic sensors under the robot detect a magnetic field in the floor and help keep the robot on track.

3. The path for the robot is easy to install as it is simply a white line on the floor.

Answers *continued*

4. Complete this table about the tools on robot arms in a car factory

Tool	Use
Spray gun	painting
Suction tool	Picking up car windscreens
Welding gun	welding

5. They are an inexpensive and safe way to train people to use expensive equipment.

6. Training people, creating 3D plans and designs, and games and leisure pursuits.

7. Because they react instantly to the data fed to them by the sensors.

8. Writing programs to control automated systems.

9. Since the software is on ROM chips it does not need to be loaded in from backing storage.

10. Embedded systems are used in cars and mobile phones.

11. It has sensors that enable it to 'hear' and 'see' and has its own processor and memory.

12. Installing hardware, maintaining software.

13. Paying for robots, paying for a systems analyst, building a new factory, training programs.

14. In the long term they save money because they become more efficient.

15. Replacing a robot arm or a computer system with the latest model.

16. Decide where the robot arms should go, where the paths for the mobile robots should be, whether to use cables or wireless to communicate with the robots, what safety measures are needed.

INDEX

Page numbers in italics indicate exam questions.

Index